ISBN 978-1-331-50475-7
PIBN 10199101

1 MONTH OF FREE READING

at

www.ForgottenBooks.com

By purchasing this book you are eligible for one month membership to ForgottenBooks.com, giving you unlimited access to our entire collection of over 700,000 titles via our web site and mobile apps.

To claim your free month visit:

www.forgottenbooks.com/free199101

REPORT

$\frac{1469}{3855}$

ON THE

RGANIZATION FOR THE ADMINISTRATION OF CIVIL GOVERNMENT INSTITUTED BY EMILIO AGUINALDO AND HIS FOLLOWERS IN THE PHILIPPINE ARCHIPELAGO

U. Bureau of insular affairs

Compilation and Report
BY
JOHN R. M. TAYLOR
CAPTAIN, 14TH INFANTRY
ASSISTANT TO CHIEF OF BUREAU OF INSULAR AFFAIRS
WAR DEPARTMENT
SEPTEMBER 5, 1903

WASHINGTON
GOVERNMENT PRINTING OFFICE
1903.

WAR DEPARTMENT
Document No. 210
Bureau of Insular Affairs

WAR DEPARTMENT,
BUREAU OF INSULAR AFFAIRS,
Washington, D. C., September 5, 1903.

SIR: Agreeable to your special direction, I have the honor to transmit herewith the report respecting the organizations for the administration of the affairs of the civil government instituted by Emilio Aguinaldo and his followers in the Philippine Archipelago, prepared by Capt. John R. M. Taylor, in charge of records relating to the Philippine insurrection, deposited with this Bureau.

Very respectfully,

CLARENCE R. EDWARDS,
Colonel, U. S. Army, Chief of Bureau.

The honorable the SECRETARY OF WAR.

(Accompanying report by Captain Taylor.)

3

REPORT ON PHILIPPINE GOVERNMENT.

WAR DEPARTMENT,
BUREAU OF INSULAR AFFAIRS,
Washington, D. C., August 26, 1903.

SIR: I have the honor to submit the following report respecting the organizations for the administration of the affairs of civil government instituted by Emilio Aguinaldo and his followers in the Philippine Archipelago.

The information utilized in preparing this report is a mass of records captured from the Philippine insurgents during the period of hostilities. These are now on file in the Bureau of Insular Affairs of the War Department. There are, necessarily, breaks in the continuity of the record, but there are about 120,000 documents, letters, drafts of decrees, and order books, which more or less completely cover the whole period of the insurrection. I have made myself acquainted with the contents of these papers, and statements of fact made herein are based upon the original records of the insurgents. Where a document is quoted, a translation of which has been published in an official publication of the United States Government, and is therefore accessible, citation thereto will be made.

From May 1, 1898, the United States fleet controlled the waters of Luzon. The Spanish governor-general had left the portion of his command outside of Manila in small detachments, too far apart for mutual support and too small to suppress revolt, except in the towns they watched. When war was declared he had been in the islands for only three months. He was wrought upon to believe that the insurrection of 1896–97 was suppressed and forgotten. The Spanish governor-general was empowered to grant measures of reform. The Spanish Government had given him the fullest power to take such action as would, in case of an attack by a United States force, unite the people and save the Philippines to Spain. He called for volunteers on May 4. Native volunteers had been employed with success by his predecessor in his operations against Aguinaldo, but no just estimate seems to have been placed upon the blow to Spanish prestige caused by the destruction of the fleet, or the far-reaching influence of the intrigues of the Hongkong junta, who realized that to use the

Spaniards and the Americans for their own purposes would give a chance for success which would never come again. Their influence must have been exerted to induce those in correspondence with them to join the Spanish forces as a means of obtaining arms.

The response was immediate. Men who had served under Aguinaldo in 1896–97 and had seen him going into exile with what rumor reported was a princely fortune, while they had received nothing, raised battalions. Men who had served as go-betweens in the tortuous negotiations which led up to Aguinaldo's exile, and who had, according to all reports, profited by those negotiations and were ready to profit by new ones, offered their unconditional adherence to the cause of Spain. These volunteers were immediately armed and equipped by the Spanish military authorities and marched to take position in the lines defending Manila. If there had been no previous understanding with Aguinaldo, certainly negotiations with his emissaries, who arrived with Admiral Dewey, were begun by the commanders of volunteers almost as soon as they took their place in line.

(Exhibit A, p. 19.) Aguinaldo arrived at Cavite May 19, 1898. The first desertion to him from the Spanish forces took place on May 23. It was a battalion of volunteers, enlisted in Pampanga Province, which had reached Manila April 29, 1898, and had been stationed between Manila and Bacoor, a town near Cavite. Almost immediately the greater part of the remaining native volunteers passed, with their arms, to Aguinaldo. The loyal troops had to fall back to the line of blockhouses which had been built in March, 1898, about Manila, in view of a possible conflict with the United States.

By May 29 Manila was blockaded by the United States fleet in the bay and by the insurgent forces on land. The Spanish command there consisted of Spanish and native troops, but the native troops were the old native regiments, part of the Spanish Philippine army. As a whole they and the civil guard remained true to their colors and did not join the insurgents until disbanded by the Spanish Government after the fall of Manila. Some never did join the insurrection. According to a general order of the Spanish governor, on May 29, 1898, there were in Manila 6,760 Spanish and 4,332 native soldiers of the Spanish army, total of 11,092, to defend a city of 300,000 people, covered on the land side by a line of works extending some 12 miles.

The Spanish force outside of Manila amounted to about 9,000 Spanish soldiers and some native troops. In the Visayas the Spaniards concentrated, and few, if any of them, were taken prisoners; but in Luzon, where the strongest force was stationed, this was not the case. News traveled slowly in that country, with few and bad roads; no orders were issued to concentrate, to fall back on Manila; the movement of the garrisons was hampered by the presence of women and priests; the usual means of communication with Manila—the sea—

was cut off by the presence of the United States squadron in Manila Bay; transportation was difficult to obtain. Old chiefs under Aguinaldo, who had been leading the lives of banditti in the hills, descended to the valleys, and in a few weeks after Aguinaldo's arrival from Hongkong, central Luzon was in the hands of the insurgents. By August, 1898, the Spanish garrisons and Spanish civil officials in Luzon had surrendered to or been captured by the insurgents, usually with no or little resistance. One general abandoned his command and fled in a native boat to Manila by sea. Another surrendered 2,500 men. At one place the insurgents reported that they had obtained 2,000,000 rounds of ammunition; at others they obtained rifles. It was not long before the arms of the Spanish garrisons and the arms of the native volunteers were at the disposal of Aguinaldo, and with these in his hands he was in a position to dictate such form of government as he desired to the people of the islands. The terms of the capitulation of Manila, August 13, 1898, gave him a free hand, as it confined the American forces to the limits of that city; and as the status was still one of war, no reenforcements could be sent to the Philippines, still Spanish territory, to put down the insurrection against Spain.

By the capitulation of Manila half of the Spanish garrison of the Philippines was held in Manila as prisoners of the United States. The ports of Luzon were rapidly occupied by the insurgents and their garrisons seized, for the sea was held by the United States, and the Spanish gunboats which would have covered the embarkation of those garrisons had fallen into the hands of the United States or else had been concentrated in the waters of the Visayas. After August 13, 1898, the Spanish garrisons in Luzon found themselves under the alternative of surrendering to the insurgents with small or no loss, or of fighting their way back to Manila with their movements hampered by the presence of their families and by that of unarmed civilians, of suffering heavy loss, only to surrender there to the Americans. They knew the Filipinos. Promises were made to them which were not kept, and they chose what at that time seemed the easier way—surrender to the insurgents. The exigency of the situation confined the forces of the United States to Manila. The victory of Manila Bay had destroyed the naval forces by which Spain controlled the seaways of the archipelago. These were the conditions under which Aguinaldo was enabled to establish his government. He could not have done it without the presence of the forces of the United States, forces which Aguinaldo at first assured the people of Luzon and the Spaniards were absolutely at his disposal. Subsequently, when he had obtained from their presence all that he had hoped for, he found it to his advantage to state that they would be as easily beaten by him as had been the scattered troops of Spain.

When Emilio Aguinaldo landed at Cavite he was immediately surrounded by the disaffected. About him gathered all who had been forced to conceal old hates, old rancors against Spanish officials, all who had dreamed of independence for the Philippines, and most of those who hoped—for even then there were natives who so hoped—that the United States would take possession of the Philippine Archipelago.

(Exhibit A, p. 19.) On May 24 he issued a proclamation, proclaiming himself dictator and promising to resign his power into the hands of a president and cabinet, who would be appointed at such time as a constitutional assembly should be convened, which would be when the islands had passed into his control. He further announced that the North American Nation had given its disinterested protection in order that the liberty of the Philippines should be gained.

Some of the men who gathered about him were trained in the law; some had served the Spanish Government in various capacities. They were accustomed to the methods of government in the Philippines, and were ready to draw up constitutions and regulations for the new government.

The following organic decrees were promulgated by the dictator:

(Exhibit B, p. 20.) Cavite, June 18, 1898, providing for election of municipal officials.

(Exhibit C, p. 22.) Regulations for provinces and municipalities, Cavite, June 20, 1898.

(Exhibit D, p. 29.) Proclamation proclaiming the revolutionary government, Cavite, June 23, 1898.

DECREE OF JUNE 18, 1898.

In brief, this provided that as soon as the territory of the archipelago, or any portion thereof, had passed from the possession of Spanish forces the people in the towns who were most conspicuous for their intelligence, social position, and upright conduct were to meet and elect a town government. The heads of the towns in every province were to elect a head for the province and his three councilors. The provincial council, composed of these four officials, with the presidente of the capital of the province, were to see to the execution in that province of the decrees of the central government and to advise and suggest.

This provincial council was to elect representatives for the revolutionary congress, which was to be charged with submitting suggestions to the central government upon interior and exterior affairs, and it was to be heard by the government upon serious matters which admitted of delay and discussion. Before any person elected to office was permitted to discharge his functions, his election was to be approved by the central government. The military commanders, except in time of war, were to have no jurisdiction over the civil authorities. They could, however, demand such supplies as they might need, and these could not be refused. The government was to appoint commissioners to carry these regulations into effect.

DECREE OF JUNE 20, 1898.

Police.—The head of the town was to organize a force of police as large as the resources of the town permitted. The commissioner of police was to command this force. He was to have the rank of lieutenant in the army. This force was to be under the command of the head of the town and of the province. The military commanders were to be able to use these police in case of necessity. All men over 18 could be called upon to serve in this force.

Justice.—The head of the town was to act as a judge and make the preliminary investigation in case of crime or suit between persons of his jurisdiction, and take testimony in such cases. The evidence was to be transmitted to the provincial council, which was to appoint an attorney to examine it and those presumed to be guilty. The papers in the case were to be referred to the provincial council, which was to call the accused before it, hear what they had to say in their defense, and pronounce sentence. This part of the trial was to be in public. The Spanish penal code, when not opposed to the decrees of the government, was to remain in force until the complete triumph of the revolution. Courts-martial were to have jurisdiction over the members of the militia of the revolution, police called upon for service by the military commanders of the provinces, and also persons committing such offenses as the government might designate in the future for trial by court-martial.

Civil causes were to be adjudicated first by the municipal councils and then by the provincial councils on appeal. These cases could be taken up on appeal by tribunals of competent jurisdiction, when, after the proclamation of the republic, a system of administering justice was completely organized. The Spanish civil code was to remain provisionally in force.

Concerning taxation and registration of property.—As soon as the popular organization was established, according to the decree of June 18, the head of the town was to take possession of all property belonging to the town and also that left by the Spaniards and was to proceed to administer it for the greatest benefit of all. All local taxes established by the Spanish Government were to be continued in force, except that gambling was forbidden. Product of fines was to be turned into the treasury of the town. This section provides also for collection of taxes. The central government was to have the right of imposing special taxes when it saw fit, the amount to be determined by the said government after hearing the representatives of the province in the matter, if there were representatives of the province. The secretary of the treasury was charged with the collection and accounting for said sums. Estimates of receipts and expenses of each town were to be drawn up and submitted through the provincial government to the central government for its approval. The towns were to be allowed to retain in their treasuries only an amount sufficient to cover their expenses as estimated; all excess was to be turned over to the provincial treasury. The provincial governments were to draw up immediately an estimate of receipts and expenditures. These were to be submitted for approval to the central government. All amounts received in excess of estimated expenses were to be turned over to the central treasury. A return of all real property, with the names of owners of the same and the amount produced by the same, was to be drawn up in each town.

DECREE OF JUNE 23, 1898.

The revolutionary government.—The dictatorial government was in future to be entitled the revolutionary government. Its duty was to struggle for the independence of the Philippines in order to establish a true republic. The dictator was in future to be called the President of the revolutionary government. There were to be four secretaries of the government—one of foreign affairs, commerce, and marine; one of war and public works; one of police and interior order, justice, education, and hygiene; one of the treasury, agriculture, and manufactures. The government could increase the number if necessary. The secretaries were to assist the president in the dispatch of business coming under their departments.

The revolutionary congress.—This was to be composed of representatives from the provinces of the Philippine Archipelago, elected as provided by the decree of June 18. In case a province was not able to elect representatives, the government would appoint them for such province. The congress was to discuss and advise, to approve treaties and loans, examine and approve the accounts of the secretary of the treasury. In case important matters admitted of delay, the congress would be heard concerning them, but if they did not admit of delay, the president of the government was to act at once. Projects of law could be presented by any representative and by the secretaries of the government. A permanent committee of congress presided over by the vice-president was to be chosen by that body. This was to serve as a court of appeal in criminal cases and as a court of final jurisdiction in cases arising between secretaries of the government and provincial officials. The acts of congress were not to go into effect until the president of the government ordered their execution. He was also to have the right of veto.

In short, the president of the revolutionary government had all the power of the Spanish governor-general, unhampered by any orders from Spain. The scheme provided for the eventual formation of a republic, but it is doubtful whether the people who drew it up knew what the word meant. What was provided for was a strong and highly centralized military dictatorship, in which, under the form of election, provision was made for the filling of all offices by men devoted to the group which had seized the functions of government.

This form of government was carried into effect as rapidly as territory was won from the Spaniards. It was a well-devised plan to secure complete control for the central groups about Aguinaldo. His commissioners, by a pretended election, in which the electors were picked men, established municipal governments devoted to the cause of the revolution. These were to choose provincial officials and members of the congress. But all elections were subject to Aguinaldo's approval, and every province was under the command of a military representative of Aguinaldo, who could call at any time upon the civil authorities for such supplies as he deemed fit. All real power was vested in the central group, and the central group was composed of Emilio Aguinaldo and his public and private advisers. The congress could advise. There is nothing in the papers on file in this office to show that it ever did anything except discuss the constitution. The government was carried on by decrees issued by Aguinaldo, and there is everything to show that these were enforced up to the time when the members of the central group were scattered by the advance of the forces of the United States in 1899.

The papers on file in this office throw a light upon the methods employed in the organization of the new government. As the Spanish garrisons fell as prisoners into the hands of Aguinaldo's forces, his commissioners held the elections for municipal and provincial officials prescribed in his decree of June 18. In every case the commissioner was appointed by Aguinaldo, usually from the military commanders in the province where the election was to be held. The commissioner chose the electors, apparently suggested the persons to be elected, presided at the election, and forwarded a record of the proceedings to the central government. The act had to be approved by the dictator, or president, before the successful candidate could assume the duties of his office. The people were not consulted. They were not in the habit of being consulted, and probably saw no necessity therefor.

Aguinaldo usually approved the decision of his representative. There are some cases of record here where he disapproved for informality in conducting the election. One case of informality which led to his disapproval of the election was that the presidente who had been certified to him as elected was reported to have been on good terms with the Spanish authorities of the town. The returns on file here show how many votes were cast in the elections. In the town of Lipa, Batangas Province, with a population of 40,733, at the election held July 3, 1898, a presidente was chosen for the town; 25 votes were cast for him. On November 23, 1898, at an election held at Vigan, Ilocos Sur, for presidente, to succeed one who had been elected representative in congress, 116 votes were cast. The population of Vigan is 19,000. October 5, 1898, at an election held at Gamu, Isabela Province, 72 votes elected a presidente. The population of Gamu is 6,101. October 7, 1898, at Echague, Isabela Province, a presidente was elected for whom 54 votes were cast. The population is 5,400. October 2, 1898, at Cabagan Nuevo, Isabela, 111 men voted out of a population of 6,240.

(Exhibit E, p. 34.) As an example of the official records of these elections, I have had translated one of an election held in Balayan, Batangas Province. Those on record in this office are all of nearly the same form. In substance they are the same.

These elections, so-called, were not always held without protest. For example, the town of San Jose, Batangas, protested unavailingly to Aguinaldo against the result of an election held at 10 p. m. in a storm of rain being considered valid. Men who had been on friendly terms with the Spaniards were usually excluded from all participation. From these acts of election it is evident that the commissioner appointed to supervise really chose the municipal authorities; a limited group of adherents confirmed his selection.

The Spanish law, known as the Maura law, which regulated the elections in the municipalities under the Spanish Government provided for a limited electoral body, composed largely of exofficials of the municipality; so, doubtlesss, this electoral body, chosen by the military commander of a district, did not seem strange to the people. The number of electors evidently depended upon the will of the commissioner appointed to hold the election. Some commissioners delegated their functions to others. There are here records showing several cases of lieutenants appointed commissioners, and, by this process of election I have described, selecting the members of municipal governments.

By December, 1898, municipal governments devoted, or supposed to be devoted, to the cause of the revolution had been established throughout the island of Luzon. It is probable that not a few of the heads of these municipalities were opposed to the methods pursued by the masters of the revolution. There are quantities of complaints among these papers of the conduct of the soldiers who were quartered upon them, of the abuses committed by the functionaries who traveled through the towns, receiving food, lodging, and transportation, and paying nothing. A number of the presidentes, or heads of municipalities, tried to resign, the number of resignations increasing rapidly in January, 1899, perhaps owing to an increasing distrust of the party in power, which was preparing for war with the United States. But it was not easy for the head of a town under the revolutionary government to resign. He had to prove by medical certificates that he was physically unable to discharge the duties of his office.

(Exhibit F, p. 35.) As soon as the municipalities had been organized, under adherents of the revolution, the provinces were organized. There are records here showing that the local presidentes of Bataan Province met on August 13, 1898, at Cavite Viejo, Cavite Province, under the presidency of Tomás Tirona, commissioner of Aguinaldo, who was then at Bacoor only 4 miles away, to elect the officials of Bataan Province. On August 9, 1898, an election was held at Bacoor for the provincial government of Pampanga Province. This election was presided over by the secretary of the interior of Aguinaldo's cabinet. On December 22, 1898, the presidentes of 41 towns of the provinces of Ambos Camarines met at Malolos under the presidency of the secretary of the interior to elect provincial officials. The election of these officials was formally approved by Aguinaldo. Taking place, as they did, under the supervision of his representatives and either at his seat of government or in immediate proximity thereto, these elections must have insured a provincial council devoted to the cause represented by Aguinaldo. I have not found the records of provincial elections in other provinces, but provincial governments existed there and probably were chosen under similar conditions.

The government thus constituted excited opposition in Pangasinán and Tarlac provinces, and the opposition to it had to be suppressed by armed force. The provinces of Ilocos and Cagayan were taken possession of by an armed expedition which sailed from Manila Bay in the summer of 1898. But the leaders of the insurrection held the arms, and Aguinaldo in a circular letter addressed to the foreign consuls in Manila on August 6, 1898, urging the recognition of his force then in rebellion against Spain, stated:[a]

The government of the revolution actually rules in the provinces of Cavite, Batangas, Mindoro, Tayabas, Laguna, Morong, Bulacan, Bataan, Pampanga, Infanta, and besieges the capital, Manila. The most perfect order and tranquillity reign in these provinces, governed by authorities elected by the inhabitants in conformity with the organic decrees dated June 18 and 23 last. Moreover, the revolution has about 9,000 prisoners of war, who are treated humanely and according to the rules of civilized warfare. We can muster more than 30,000 men, organized as a regular army.

On August 7 he wrote[a] that there were agents of the revolutionary government in Japan and England and France, and one was about to start for the United States. In a decree dated Bacoor, August 10,

---

[a] Letter sent book of the secretary of foreign affairs of the insurgent government on file in Bureau of Insular Affairs, War Department,

1898, Aguinaldo specified the powers and functions of the Hongkong Junta, which was empowered to represent his government abroad, disposing of certain sums in its possession for the purchase of arms, and to act as a center of intrigue in Europe and the United States. The foreign agents reported to the government of Aguinaldo through the Hongkong Junta.

In order to show the scope of the control exercised over the municipal and provincial authorities constituted, as I have already shown, I have had briefs made of a collection of decrees of the president and of the orders and letters of the secretary of the interior of the insurgent government, contained in a record book formerly part of the records of the latter official. This volume, now on file in this office, covers the period of July 16, 1898, to October 2, 1899.

Exhibit G (p. 37) contains a brief of all in this collection which is pertinent to the present subject. They are not all that were issued, but they are sufficient to show that an effective control was insured.

From the papers of municipalities and of provinces on file here it is evident that at least an attempt was made to comply with the provisions of the orders herein contained, and that failure to execute completely was more often due to want of ability, or to disturbed conditions produced by war, than to want of zeal. The islands under the control of Aguinaldo were governed like a besieged city, by the will of the commanding officer, and his will was expressed by decrees or the orders and instructions issued by the secretaries of his cabinet, or, what probably more accurately describes it, his council of government.

After the adoption of the constitution the more important decrees of the president begin with some such form as "Upon the recommendation of the secretary of the interior, concurred in by my council, I hereby decree, etc.," and the decrees so issued were countersigned by the secretary within whose province the matter came, or by the secretary of the council. But this change in the form of issuing decrees is the only change which I have been able to discover was made in the methods of government by the adoption of the constitution. The Filipino conception of a republic was apparently the Spanish government of the Philippines, with a native at the head who was to exercise, under the title of president, all the powers of a governor-general and captain-general, unhampered by any possibility of an appeal to Spain.

(Exhibit H, p. 51.) As long as the conditions permitted, the orders of the government were promulgated by being printed in the official publication, El Heraldo de la Revolución, the name of which was subsequently changed to Gaceta de Filipinas. This paper had the official character of the Gaceta de Manila, published under the Spanish Government, and was by a decree of Aguinaldo required to be subscribed to by officials whose duties required them to be cognizant of information contained therein. A translation of this decree appears in the exhibits, with a reproduction of the first number of the Gaceta de Filipinas, dated May 17, 1899. The original is on file in this office.

The power of Aguinaldo was at its height in January, 1899. Luzon was in his hands, and the great island of Panay had recognized his government. An armed expedition had sailed to overturn the government which had been formed by the Visayans and substitute that of "The Federal State of the Visayas" by the "Politico-Military Government of Panay," with one of Aguinaldo's generals at its head. Except in Negros and the greater part of Mindanao, the Sulu Archipelago, Manila, and Cavite, the decrees of Aguinaldo were obeyed, and, although this obedience may not have been implicit, yet these decrees were held as expressing the will of the supreme power. They were the expression of the will of the only government which claimed supremacy. The men who brought them came with arms, the only firearms in the islands except among the Moros, and coming from Luzon, the seat of Spanish power, they were accepted. An artful campaign of propaganda, supported by a system of terrorism was carried on, and, whatever may have been the methods by which that supremacy was obtained, an examination of these records shows that at that time, except in the territory named, the government of Aguinaldo was supreme in the archipelago.

On January 4, 1899, Major-General Otis, military governor in the Philippines, issued a proclamation [a] in which he quoted instructions from the President of the United States, which showed that the United States intended to extend its authority over the Philippine Archipelago. Aguinaldo replied at once by the proclamation, a translation of which is given (Exhibit I, p. 53). I remember that these proclamations were posted during the night of, I think, January 6, on the walls and doors of Manila, and remained posted near the proclamation of the military governor until removed in the morning by the soldiers of the provost-guard. On February 5, 1899, after the attack on Manila, he formally declared war.

On January 21, 1899, the constitution [b] of the so-called republic was approved by Aguinaldo, but there is nothing to show that it was enforced. To the time of its final disintegration the government was conducted in accordance with the fundamental decrees of June 18, 1898, as affected by subsequent decrees of Aguinaldo.

(Exhibit J, p. 56.) The ability to levy and collect taxes is probably

---

[a] Printed page 68, Report of Maj. Gen. E. S. Otis, on Military Operations and Civil Affairs in the Philippine Islands, 1899.

[b] Translation printed page 189, Report of the Philippine Commission to the President, vol. 1, January 31, 1900.

the ultimate test of the existence of a government. I have had the account books of the insurgent government in this office balanced, and extracts made from the accounts which are of interest. These books cover the period from May 31, 1898, to September 10, 1899. It is not probable that the sums given in these books are the total amounts collected, for there are discrepancies between stub receipts and rough cash books and other preliminary documents and the final entries in the general ledgers covering the same period, the total of which amounts to 530,467.82 pesos. Adding this to the amounts duly credited gives a total cash collection for that period of 2,586,733.48 pesos. Some of these discrepancies may be accounted for by seizures by the United States authorities of sums in transit to the insurgent treasury. This amount is charged to the provinces and islands of Albay, Abra, Batanes Islands, Bataan, Batangas, Babuyanes Islands, Benguet, Bulacan, Camarines, Cagayan, Cavite, Cebu, Ilocos Norte, Ilocos Sur, Lepanto, Laguna, Leyte Island, Isabela, Infanta, Masbate Island, Marinduque, Morong, Mindanao Island, Mindoro Island, Manila, Nneva Ecija, Nueva Viscaya, Negros Island, Panay Island, Pampanga, Pangasinan, Romblon Island, Sorsogon, Samar Island, Tayabas, Tarlac, Union, Zambales.

In some of these the amounts reported as collected are small, so small as to show that Mindanao and Negros, for example, were not under the insurgent system, even if it were not clear from other documents on file here, but the remainder of the Christian portions of the archipelago, were under the control of the insurgent government, which appointed officials and laid and collected taxes.

The plan to be pursued in the financial administration of the government is contained in a decree dated Malolos, February 12, 1899, in which the President puts in force a scheme submitted to him by his Secretary of the Treasury. This is an elaborate estimate of receipts and expenses for the year, and is based upon the Spanish budget or "presupuesto" for the Philippines. The translation of the letter submitting the project of the law or decree, and the law itself, which appear in the exhibits, show the methods of making collections for the government and of maintaining a system of accountability. In the translation the estimate of expenses and receipts, and the allowances to be made from the receipts of the treasury for the maintenance of the different branches of the government, have been omitted. The fact of war with the United States, and perhaps dishonesty among the agents of the government, prevented the receipts being as great as had been estimated upon, but the papers on file in this office show that this decree was constantly referred to, and that allotments of funds were as far as possible made in accordance with its provisions. (Exhibit L, p. 68.)

The officials appointed by the government of Aguinaldo were recognized as representatives of a government, of the government of the the archipelago outside of Manila, not only by the people of the islands, but by the foreign merchants domiciled in Manila and trading to the parts of the islands. This recognition is shown by applications by the managers and authorized agents of such houses to trade, by their payment of customs duties at ports held by the insurgents, to their authorized officials, not as a forced contribution of war or an exaction, but as a duly laid customs duty acquiesced in by the payer.

(Exhibit K, p. 56.) The manager of the Compañía Marítima, of Manila, the largest shipping firm then in the islands, on January 25, 1899, paid 1,506.68 pesos to the president of the revolutionary government for licenses for five vessels to engage in coastwise trade. The stubs of these licenses, certified to by E. Aguinaldo's initials written by him, are on file in this office in a record book of licenses issued, filed under 04.

(Exhibit K, p. 56.) The relations of the foreign merchants in Manila with the insurgents can best be seen by the abstract I have prepared of documents among these records. It would be idle to hope to find all the correspondence on a subject of such magnitude and character, but Exhibit K, composed of briefs and documents the originals of which are on file in this Bureau, shows that many, perhaps all of the foreign merchants domiciled in Manila under the protection of the American flag, procured licenses from and paid customs duties to the revolutionary organization. That many of them were also war traitors is proven by the evidence, which shows that their agents bought produce, chiefly hemp, from insurgent leaders then in the field against the United States, said hemp having been seized by those leaders as a contribution of war; the money received from the sale of which would insure their ability to continue the campaign.

Exhibit K, p. 56, gives extracts showing how foreign merchants domiciled in Manila paid customs duties to the insurgent government. Their agents in the provinces also paid contributions to the insurgent treasury, as shown in Exhibit M, p. 77. All men of property were called upon by the insurgents to contribute according to their means to the expenses of the war.

A report of cash received shows 385,332.53 pesos received as contributions of war between May 31, 1898, and February 27, 1899, by the central government. This record is probably of cash contributions. The contributions called for were usually paid in kind. Long reports are on file among these papers giving detailed statements of what had been turned over to the collecting agents—rice, horses, clothes, everything which could be of use. The paying of taxes in kind was nothing strange or unusual. The earliest "tribute" to the Spanish Government was paid in kind. On the church estates rents were frequently paid in produce, and in the hemp-growing provinces hemp would be the article most eagerly taken up by the tax collectors as meeting the most ready sale. The sale of hemp in the southern provinces of Luzon undoubtedly prolonged the insurrection there.

Other sources of revenue of the insurgent government were a national loan, authorized by a decree of the president. The total amount authorized was 20,000,000 pesos. Apparently, at least, bonds for 500,000 pesos were printed, divided into two series: A, of 25,000 bonds of 100 pesos each, and B, of 100,000 bonds of 25 pesos each, making a total of 500,000 pesos. Interest was to be at 6 per cent. This loan was to be subscribed for by all persons of means, and pressure was placed upon them, insuring that they should subscribe. There were large sums collected by government agents and collected in the name of the government. There were large losses, some possibly by peculation, before the amounts collected reached the central government, but some amounts reached the treasury; for example, on October 19, 1899, a total amount of 233,397.50 pesos is reputed as having been received from the installments to be paid by subscribers up to that date. But a preliminary cash book shows 388,650 pesos paid from the same source up to September, 1899, six weeks before. Even making allowance for books kept upon the single-entry system, such a difference is at the least suspicious, and there is every reason for believing that a larger sum must have been originally collected by the agents of the insurgent government. These sums were collected throughout Luzon by agents of the insurgent government duly authorized for that purpose, receipts were given, and sums accounted for on forms issued by the insurgent government.

These records show that stamps were printed and used on correspondence where postal routes were organized, that revenue stamps were required upon paper certifying to transfer of cattle and real estate, that telegrams had to be stamped, and that a system of stamped paper for official and legal documents similar to that employed by the Spanish Government was adopted. There are among the records in this Bureau stamped envelopes which have passed through the insurgent post and documents of various kinds drawn up upon stamped paper issued by the insurgent government, sufficient in volume and extent to establish the fact that a considerable sum must have been derived from their sales. From May 31, 1898, to February 15, 1899, 102,940.60 pesos were received from postage and telegraph stamps.

Steps were taken to restore the Spanish system of forestry control, licenses were issued to cut wood, and officials of the forestry department appointed.

These original papers on file here show that the insurgent government, under the various names Dictatorship, Revolutionary Government, Republic, which it assumed at the will of its leaders, exercised many, if not all, the powers of a de facto government. That it was not recognized does not affect the statement. Until it was disintegrated under the shattering blows of the forces of the United States, it raised armies, laid and collected taxes and customs duties, provided for trial by process of law of both civil and criminal cases, provided for a postal and telegraph system, and chose officials for its civil government by a method which, however little it may have considered the desires and aspirations of the governed, was yet effective and orderly in its action.

While the documents which I have cited would indicate a civil government providing for equality of right and privilege, yet the documents on file in this Bureau showing its methods prove it to have been in fact a military dictatorship. Its extent and its methods were necessarily unknown until these papers were examined.

Specious as are in appearance some of these orders and decrees, yet further consultation of the records captured from the insurgents in the Philippines shows that behind them assassination was employed as an effective addition to political propaganda and murder as an ultimate resource in political maneuvres.

I am, sir, very respectfully, your obedient servant,

JOHN R. M. TAYLOR,
Captain Fourteenth Infantry,
Assistant to the Chief of the Bureau of Insular Affairs.

The CHIEF OF THE BUREAU OF INSULAR AFFAIRS,
War Department, Washington, D. C.

A.

[Original filed No. 1¹, Philippine Insurgent Records.]

[Translation.]

MY BELOVED COUNTRYMEN: I accepted the agreement of peace proposed by Don Pedro A. Paterno after his consultation with the Captain-General of the islands (Philippines), agreeing in consequence thereof to surrender our arms and disband the troops under my immediate command under certain conditions, as I believed it more advantageous for the country than to sustain the insurrection, for which I had but limited resources, but as some of the said conditions were not complied with, some of the bands are discontented and have not surrendered their arms. Five months have elapsed without the inauguration of any of the reforms which I asked in order to place our country on a level with civilized people—for instance, our neighbor, Japan, which in the short space of twenty years has reached a point where she has no reason to envy anyone, her strength and ascendency being shown in the last war with China. I see the impotence of the Spanish Government to contend with certain elements which oppose constant obstacles to the progress of the country itself and whose destructive influence has been one of the causes of the uprising of the masses, and as the great and powerful North American nation has offered its disinterested protection to secure the liberty of this country, I again assume command of all the troops in the struggle for the attainment of our lofty aspirations, inaugurating a dictatorial government to be administered by decrees promulgated under my sole responsibility and with the advice of distinguished persons until the time when these islands, being under our complete control, may form a constitutional republican assembly and appoint a president and cabinet, into whose hands I shall then resign the command of the islands.

Given at Cavite, May 24, 1898.

EMILIO AGUINALDO.

B.

[Printed in Senate Doc. 62, part 1, 55th Cong., 3d sess, 1898-99, pp. 432-437.]

Aguinaldo's proclamation of June 18, 1898, establishing the dictatorial government.

To the Philippine public:

Circumstances have providentially placed me in a position for which I can not fail to recognize that I am not properly qualified; but since I can not violate the laws of Providence nor decline the obligations which honor and patriotism impose upon me, I now salute you, oh, my beloved people.

I have proclaimed in the face of the whole world that the aspiration of my whole life, the final object of all my efforts and strength, is nothing else but your independence, for I am firmly convinced that that constitutes your constant desire, and that independence signifies for us redemption from slavery and tyranny, regaining our liberty and entrance into the concert of civilized nations.

I understand, on the other hand, that the first duty of every government is to faithfully interpret popular aspirations; with this motive, although the abnormal circumstances of the war have compelled me to institute this dictatorial government which assumes full powers, both civil and military, my constant desire is to surround myself with the most distinguished persons of each province, those that by their conduct deserve the confidence of their province, to the end that the true necessities of each being known by them, measures may be adopted to meet those necessities and apply the remedies in accordance with the desires of all.

I understand, moreover, the urgent necessity of establishing in each town a solid and robust organization, the strongest bulwark of public security and the sole means of securing that union and discipline which are indispensable for the establishment of the republic, that is, government of the people for the people, and warding off the international conflicts which may arise.

Following out the foregoing considerations, I decree as follows:

ARTICLE I. The inhabitants of every town where the forces of the Spanish Government still remain will decide upon the most efficacious measures to combat and destroy them, according to the resources and means at their disposal, according to prisoners of war the treatment most conformable to humanitarian sentiments and to the customs observed by civilized nations.

Art. II. As soon as the town is freed from Spanish domination, the inhabitants most distinguished for high character, social position, and honorable conduct, both in the center of the community and in the suburbs, will come together in a large meeting, in which they will proceed to elect, by a majority of votes, the chief of the town and a headman for each suburb, considering as suburbs not only those hitherto known as such, but also the center of the community.

All those inhabitants who fulfill the conditions above named will have the right to take part in this meeting and to be elected, provided always that they are friendly to the Philippine independence and are 20 years of age.

Art. III. In this meeting shall also be elected, by a majority of votes, three delegates, one of police and internal order, another of justice and civil registry, and another of taxes and property.

The delegate of justice and civil registry will aid the chief in the formation of courts and in keeping of books of registry, of births, deaths, and marriage contracts, and of the census.

The delegates of taxes and property will aid the chief in the collection of taxes and administration of public funds, the opening of books of registry of cattle and real property, and all work relating to encouragement of every class of industry.

Art. IV. The chief, as president, with the headman and the above-mentioned delegates, will constitute the popular assemblies, who will supervise the exact fulfillment of the laws in force and the particular interests of each town.

The headman of the center of the community will be the vice-president of the assembly and the delegate of justice its secretary.

. The headmen will be delegates of the chief within their respective boundaries.

Art. V. The chiefs of each town, after consulting the opinion of their respective assemblies, will meet and elect by a majority of votes the chief of the province and three councilors for the three branches above mentioned.

The chief of the province as president, the chief of the town which is the capital of the province as vice-president, and the above-named councilors will constitute the provincial council, which will supervise the carrying out of the instructions of this government in the territory of the province and for the general interest of the province, and will propose for this government the measures which should be adopted for the general welfare.

Art. VI. The above-named chiefs will also elect by a majority of votes three representatives for each one of the provinces of Manila and Cavite, two for each one of the provinces classified as terminal in Spanish legislation, and one for each one of the other provinces and politico-military commands of the Philippine Archipelago.

The above-named representatives will guard the general interests of the archipelago and the particular interests of their respective provinces, and will constitute the revolutionary congress which will propose to this government the measures concerning the preservation of internal order and external security of these islands, and will be heard by this government on all questions of grave importance, the decision of which will admit of delay or adjournment.

Art. VII. Persons elected to any office whatsoever in the form prescribed in the preceding article can not perform the same without the previous confirmation by this government, which will give it in accordance with the certificates of election.

Representatives will establish their identity by exhibiting the above-named certificates.

ART. VIII. The military chiefs named by this government in each province will not intervene in the government and administration of the province, but will confine themselves to requesting of the chiefs of provinces and of the towns the aid which may be necessary, both in men and resources, which are not to be refused in case of actual necessity.

Nevertheless, when the province is threatened or occupied by the enemy, in whole or in part, the military chief of highest rank therein may assume the powers of the chief of the province until the danger has disappeared.

ART. IX. The government will name for each province a commissioner specially charged with establishing therein the organization prescribed in this decree in accordance with instructions which this government will communicate to him. Those military chiefs who liberate the towns from the Spanish domination are commissioners by virtue of their office.

The above-named commissioners will preside over the first meetings held in each town and in each province.

ART. X. As soon as the organization provided in the decree has been established, all previous appointments to any civil office whatsoever, no matter what their origin or source, shall be null and void, and all instructions in conflict with the foregoing are hereby annulled.

Given at Cavite the 18th day of June, 1898.

EMILIO AGUINALDO.

C.

[Original filed in No. 206-3, Philippine Insurgent Records.]

For the execution of and proper compliance with the provisions of the decree of this government concerning t e government of the provinces and towns of the Philippine Archipelago, I hereby decree the following:

As supplementary to the said decree of the 18th instant, the following instructions shall be observed concerning the administration of the provinces and towns:

OF THE HOLDING OF MEETINGS.

Rule 1.—The authority vested with powers to preside over the meetings of the juntas and of the councils shall convoke the persons constituting either of these by sending to each one a notice in writing of the day and hour, place and object of the meeting. When urgent matters are concerned a verbal message may be sent.

Rule 2.—No one shall fail to be present at the meetings without showing in writing justifiable cause which prevents it. He who fails to attend without complying with this requisite shall pay a fine of half a peso, which shall be deposited in the town treasury.

Rule 3.—Meetings shall always be held when business of a serious and important nature for the town or province is to be considered, but which is not of an urgent character. The chiefs may determine for themselves matters which are urgent, but shall communicate to the council or junta at the first meeting which may be held the decision they may have adopted. Nevertheless, the councils and juntas shall hold a meeting once a month at least.

Rule 4.—Any member of the junta or council may move any measure which may be of interest for the town or province; but the motions shall be put in clear and concise terms.

When any motion is made, the president shall invite the other members to state their opinions and briefly explain the reasons for or against, endeavoring not to waste the time in long discourses, which have no other end than to confuse the point. When the business shall have been sufficiently discussed, the president shall ask each of the members if he must or must not accept the motion, and such action shall be taken as is approved by a majority of one vote.

Rule 5.—Motions of great importance shall be previously examined by a committee appointed for the purpose, which shall read its report at the next meeting, and thereupon discussion shall be held as above stated.

Rule 6.—The meetings as well as the votings which require secrecy, on account of their importance, shall be made in secret, for which purpose two tellers shall be appointed by a majority vote and a secretary, who shall take their seats at the table at which the president is seated; then one by one the voters shall approach this table and give their vote, which the secretary shall enter on a list prepared for the purpose in the presence of said persons and the party interested. All the votes having been set down, including those of the tellers and the secretary, a recount shall be made by the same, and the result of the voting read aloud. Bribery and falsification of votes shall be checked by severe punishments.

Rule 7.—Resolutions shall not be valid without having in their favor at least three votes in the council and five in the juntas, it being well understood that said numbers constitute the only majority.

Rule 8.—The meetings shall be public, and only in those cases where secrecy is required may the meetings be held in private.

Rule 9.—Each meeting on adjournment shall prepare a minute in which shall appear a clear and succinct account of all the incidents of the meeting, and which all present shall sign. When elections are held a literal copy of the minutes shall be delivered to each one elected, signed by the members present. In every council and junta a book shall be kept wherein the minutes shall be entered in chronological order.

Rule 10.—The president shall conduct the deliberations and shall have no vote, but in case of a tie he shall have the deciding vote.

Rule 11.—Each junta shall consider the best method for establishing public schools in proportion to the means of the towns, and shall recommend the same to the council in order that it may decide what may be proper, although such decision shall be of a provisional character until the revolution triumphs.

Nevertheless, the council shall notify this government what it may decide in the matter.

OF THE FORMATION OF THE POLICE FORCE AND THE CHARACTER OF THE SAME.

Rule 12.—The chief of the town shall organize a police force, composed of armed men, in such number as the resources of the town may permit. This force shall be in charge of the police commissioner, who shall have the rank of lieutenant of the army.

Rule 13.—Said force shall carry out the orders of the chief of the town, as its immediate superior, and of the chief of the province, as superior officer of the latter, and is designed not only to maintain internal order, but also for the defense of the town.

Rule 14.—The military commanders of each province may utilize said forces in battles in case of real necessity, with the knowledge of the chief of the town, as well as of the chief of the province, if it be possible.

Rule 15.—All males from the age of eighteen years and upward are obliged to serve on said force, but enforced service shall not be required whilst volunteers offer themselves; nor are married men obliged to serve while unmarried ones are available. The ones excepted are those discharging civil functions or physically unfit.

Rule 16.—The police commissioner shall keep a book in which he shall enter not only the description of each person, but the services rendered by same. There shall be an agreement with the chief to furnish clothing for the force, and daily subsistence necessary, according to the rank of each one, which amount shall be previously fixed by the junta, and be taken from the town funds.

Rule 17.—The military commander of the province shall agree with the chief of the same and the chiefs of the respective towns as to the military instruction of the forces in question.

OF THE CONDUCT OF TRIALS, CIVIL REGISTERS, AND THE POLL.

Rule 18.—The chief of the town as judge, and the commissioner of justice as secretary, shall direct the proceedings which may be instituted against any citizen, beginning with a clear and concise statement of the act, the subject-matter of the trial, and the indispensable investigations to ascertain and secure the true culprit, concluding with a precise and categorical declaration or statement of the latter and of the witnesses for the prosecution and for the defense.

Antiquated practices and formalities which serve no other purpose than to fill papers and make the course of the trial interminable, shall be avoided.

Rule 19.—When the judge is of the opinion that there are no further investigations to be made, he shall forward the record, with the accused, to the provincial council, which shall appoint a "ponente" (see note) to examine the proceedings and report that the investigations have concluded, or that others are to be made, in the latter case giving the necessary orders to the chief of the town to supply any deficiencies observed.

Rule 20.—The proceedings having been completed the council shall order the accused to appear at a public hearing, and, after the "ponente" has read a succinct and classified statement of the process, the accused, or persons whom he may designate for his defense, shall be heard, and decision shall be pronounced after due deliberation. An appeal from this decision lies to the commission of justice to congress.

Rule 21.—The Spanish penal code, with the provisional law for the application of the provisions of the same in these islands, shall be in force provisionally until the revolution shall triumph, in so far as not opposed to the decrees of the government.

Rule 22.—Only such persons shall be tried by courts-martial who serve in the revolutionary militia and the members of the police of the towns when they shall be made use of by the military commanders of the provinces. There shall also be tried by courts-martial the principals of crimes considered as military crimes by this government in the decree which it will publish for that purpose, in view of the abnormal conditions of the war.

Rule 23.—Civil litigations, whatever the character or amounts involved, shall be decided at first instance by the juntas of the towns and at second instance by the provincial councils. The complaints and the appeals shall be presented to the chiefs of the towns and of the provinces, who shall convene the respective juntas and councils.

Either of these shall issue a decree providing for the appearance of the parties litigant with their respective evidence, and, after hearing the pleadings of each and taking the evidence offered into consideration, they shall properly deliberate and decide by majority vote on what they esteem most in accordance with justice. These decisions shall be provisional and may be amended by the tribunals of competent jurisdiction when, after the republic is proclaimed, the administration of justice shall have been duly organized.

The decisions shall conform to the provisions of the Spanish civil code, which shall likewise be in force provisionally in everything which is not in contravention with the decrees of the government.

Rule 24.—The commissioner of justice shall keep on file all the decrees and other provisions of this government.

Rule 25.—The same commissioner shall keep three books—one in which he shall enter the births, in chronological order, specifying the name of the new born, the place and day of birth, the names, surnames, and residence of the parents of the same, and, lastly, the name, surname, and residence of the godfather, who shall sign the entry as witness with the chief and the aforesaid commissioner.

Rule 26.—He shall keep another book in which he shall enter the deaths, giving the name, surname, profession, conjugal condition, and residence of the deceased, the names, surnames, and residence of the parents of the same, and the disease the cause of death.

The entry shall be signed by the chief and the commissioner, together with a witness who shall be a member of the family or a neighbor of the deceased.

Rule 27.—In the third book marriage contracts shall be entered, after conforming to the following requisites:

The contracting parties shall sign a paper stating to the chief of the town that by mutual consent they have agreed to marry, and requesting that he proceed to enter said contract in the public registry. If the contracting parties be under twenty-three years of age, their respective fathers shall subscribe the paper with them; in the absence of these, the mothers, and lacking both of these, the elder brothers, who shall have completed twenty-one years.

If none of the persons mentioned exist, authority shall be requested of the junta of the town, and this authority shall accompany the paper.

If the contracting parties have completed twenty-three years of age, a witness for each one shall subscribe the paper with them, who may be any of the parties mentioned, or another person of legal age, possessing the confidence and friendship of the interested parties. The minor contracting party who shall have obtained authority from the junta shall also be accompanied by a witness.

The document having been presented with the expressed formalities, the chief of the town shall order that the banns be published. For this purpose a notice shall be posted upon the door of the town hall, in which the aforesaid document shall be literally copied, calling upon such persons to appear who can testify and prove that either of the contracting parties has already signed a marriage contract with another person in the registry of another locality. This announcement shall likewise be read once a week in public for three consecutive weeks, such reading taking place on a holiday or market day, or some day when there is an unusual concourse of people.

When the three weeks shall have expired without any complaints having been made, those who subscribe this document shall appear before the chief and commissioner, and in the presence of the contracting parties shall state that of their own free will and by mutual consent the latter have agreed to form a conjugal union, to lead a common and indissoluble life while they live, to which end they give a formal promise of mutual fidelity, and promise to educate their children in the love of God, their neighbor, and their country. This entry shall be subscribed by all those present.

Rule 28.—If complaints be made, the contract can not be executed until it is proven that they are without foundation.

Rule 29.—No priest shall celebrate a canonical marriage unless the contracting parties present the certificate of the contract, signed by the chief and the commissioner, and if he should do so without this requisite, the marriage shall not be valid in law.

Rule 30.—Lastly, the commissioner of justice shall keep a book in which he shall make entry annually of the residents of each barrio, beginning with the town proper, stating the name, surname, conjugal condition, profession, and residence of each one, making at the end an index of the total number of souls—of the total number of men and women—of the total number of births, deaths, and marriages occurring during the year.

TAXES AND REGISTRATION OF PROPERTY.

Rule 31.—Immediately upon the establishment of the popular organization in the manner prescribed in the decree of the 18th instant and in these instructions, the chief of the town, aided by the respective commissioner, shall take charge of all the property belonging to the town, as well as that left by the Spaniards, and shall administer the same in the manner most advantageous for all in the judgment of the junta.

Rule 32.—All local taxation established by the Spanish Government shall likewise be taken in charge; exception being made of the gaming licenses and taxes on cock fighting, which are absolutely prohibited, as they cause nothing but ruin to the town and with scarcely any benefit to the public exchequer.

Rule 33.—Every kind of gambling shall be considered a crime, punishable in the code as if it were a game of chance, and the official who tolerates it shall be relieved of his office and shall pay a fine to be determined by the provincial council, in proportion to the importance of the play, but in no case shall it be less than fifty pesos.

The amount of the fines of every sort shall be deposited in the town treasury.

Rule 34.—The chief of the town, on taking charge of the above-mentioned property and taxes, shall make a detailed inventory of the same, in the following order: Money, jewels, furniture, live stock, real estate, public documents, and paper money and taxes. In this inventory the average value of each article shall be expressed, and the income derived from the real estate and taxes. A copy of this inventory, subscribed by the chief and by the commissioner, shall be sent to this government through the provincial council.

Rule 35.—The juntas may collect as an indirect local tax for each civil trial in which the amount involved is not determined, or when it is determined and does not exceed five hundred pesos, the sum of five pesos. On amounts exceeding five hundred pesos one per cent tax shall be collected. These amounts shall be paid by the losing litigant.

The councils may act in the same manner at second instance.

Rule 36.—The chiefs of towns may also demand in the manner stated the sum of one peseta for each entry of birth or death, four reales for each public notice, and twelve reales for each entry of matrimonial contract.

Rule 37.—An ordinary personal tax of one peseta per head each quarter may also be imposed upon males above the age of 18 years who do not serve in the revolútionary militia or on the police force of the town.

A special tax may also be imposed upon the well-to-do class, the amount of which shall be determined in each case by this government after hearing the opinion of the representatives of the provinces, if there should be any, when great peremptory necessities occur; but in such cases the secretary of the treasury shall circulate the statements of the collection and investment of said funds for the information and satisfaction of the taxpayers.

Rule 38.—At the beginning of each quarter the chief of the town shall order the collection of personal taxes by the heads, each of whom shall keep a book of the collections, in which he shall enter the names and surnames of those who have paid their quotas. The heads shall turn in the proceeds of the collections to the commissioner of revenue, who, after entering in the cash book the quotas collected and the names of the taxpayers, shall sign the receipt with the counter signature of the chief in the book of collections, which shall remain in the possession of the head for safekeeping.

Such persons shall be elected as councilors and commissioners of revenue who possess property sufficient to serve as security for the amounts intrusted to their care and custody.

Rule 39.—The chief of the town, with the commissioner of revenue, shall immediately formulate an estimate as to the expenses and needs of the town, and, after submitting it for the approval of the junta, shall forward it to the provincial council, which, with its report, shall forward it to this government for its definite approval.

In accordance with this estimate or budget, the chief shall adjust the expenses of the town, and the commissioner of revenue shall make no payment without the written order of the former. Pending this approval, urgent and indispensable payments may be ordered provisionally and in conformity with the same.

Rule 40.—At the end of each quarter the commissioner of revenue shall draw up the account of all disbursements made and the statement of receipts, and after examination by the junta he shall forward them to the provincial council for consolidation into a general account, which shall be forwarded to this government every six months.

Rule 41.—In the town treasury there shall be kept only an amount sufficient for the expenses of the same, in conformity with the estimate approved, the remainder being forwarded to the provincial treasury, which shall be in the custody of the councilor of revenues, under the immediate supervision of the provincial council, whose members will be jointly responsible for any defalcation which may occur.

Rule 42.—Each council on being constituted shall immediately form and submit for the approval of this government an estimate of the indispensable expenses for the provincial necessities, and the chief of the province can not order any payment except in accordance with said estimate.

The chief of the province shall order forwarded to this government any surplus funds by the safest and quickest way when called upon to do so in order to meet the general expenses of the revolution.

Rule 43.—The commissioner of revenue shall keep a book for the registration of property and the transfer of cattle. On inscribing any number of head of cattle in this register the town mark shall be branded upon the same. The certification of the entry in the registry of transfer, which the commissioner shall issue with the countersignature of the chief, will serve to establish in future the ownership of the cattle. For this work the sum of one peseta for each entry shall be demanded as a local tax.

Rule 44.—Lastly, he shall keep another book in which real estate property within the jurisdiction of each town, beginning with the town pro. er and concluding with the barrios, shall be entered. All country property, as well as city property—that is to say, the houses and lots—shall be entered by parcels, by parcels being understood the portions of ground more or less extensive which belong to one single person and occupying one site.

In the entry of each parcel its area shall be stated, its boundaries, the cultivation to which it is devoted, its approximate value, and the net annual income which may be derived therefrom. At the end shall be set the name, surname, and residence of the known owner, and if it be rented, the personal data of the tenant shall also be stated.

In the parcels which are town property, or which have no known owner, this fact shall be stated. For this work 1 per cent of the value of each parcel may be collected, the amount being paid into the town treasury.

Rule 45.—Each town may use on its official dispatches a circular seal, in the center of which a sun with eight rays, and three stars toward the upper portion, are engraved. On the upper border, besides the stars, shall be written in a semicircle the name of the province in Tagalog, and on the lower, likewise in a semicircle, the name of the town in the same language.

The councils shall use the same seal, but in place of the name of the town they shall put the word "Sangunian."

Given in Cavite, June 20, 1898.

EMILIO AGUINALDO.

The "ponente" is a judge of a tribunal of competent authority appointed by the presiding judge thereof to investigate the case at issue and the evidence submitted pro and con and advise the court whether it is pertinent thereto or not (he is appointed in turn from among the associate judges, but in case there be but two associate judges, the presiding judge also takes his turn); to verbally submit for the deliberation of the court all findings of fact and conclusions of law, and the decisions which, in his judgment, should be rendered, but without making a draft thereof; to draft the rulings and judgment in the terms agreed upon by the court, even though his vote is not in accordance with that of the majority, although, in the latter case, the presiding judge may intrust the drafting of the decision of the court to another judge if he considers it advisable by reason of special circumstances, but in any case the "ponente" may prepare a dissenting opinion; to read the judgment in open court, or in his absence the same may be read by the presiding judge; to take the depositions of witnesses and other supplementary evidence when, according to law, the same can not or should not be taken before the court ordering same, or if taken without the town where the court is sitting, and when examining judges or municipal judges are not commissioned to take such evidence; to investigate as to whether legal formalities have been observed; whether or not the instruments for which the law prescribes precise forms have been drafted in accordance therewith, or whether any abuses have been committed, either of commission or omission, in the proceedings of the action; and if there exists any mistake which should be corrected, he shall call the attention of the court thereto for the purpose of having same corrected, and procuring a strict observance of the law, in letter as well as in spirit.

On all rulings which he shall recommend to the court the "ponente" shall vote first, and afterwards the other judges in the inverse order of their seniority with regard to length of service.

D.

[Printed in Senate Doc. No. 62, part 1, 55th Cong. 3d sess., 1898–99, pp. 433–437.]

AGUINALDO'S PROCLAMATION OF JUNE 23, ESTABLISHING THE REVOLUTIONARY GOVERNMENT.

Don Emilio Aguinaldo y Famy, president of the revolutionary government of the Philippines and general in chief of its army.

This government desiring to demonstrate to the Philippine people that one of its ends is to combat with a firm hand the inveterate vices of the Spanish administration, substituting for personal luxury and that pompous ostentation which have made it a mere matter of routine, cumbrous and slow in its movements, another administration more modest, simple, and prompt in performing the public service, I decree as follows:

CHAPTER I.—*Of the revolutionary government.*

ARTICLE I. The dictatorial government will be entitled hereafter the revolutionary government, whose object is to struggle for the independence of the Philippines until all nations, including the Spanish, shall expressly recognize it, and to prepare the country so that a true republic may be established.

The dictator will be entitled hereafter president of the revolutionary government.

ART. II. Four secretaryships of government are created, one of foreign affairs, navy, and commerce; another of war and public works; another of police and internal order, justice, education, and hygiene; and another of finance, agriculture, and manufacturing industry.

The government may increase this number of secretaryships when it shall find in practice that this distribution is not sufficient for the multiplied and complicated necessities of the public service.

ART. III. Each secretaryship shall aid the president in the administration of questions concerning the different branches which it comprises.

At the head of each one shall be a secretary, who shall not be responsible for the decrees of the presidency, but shall sign them with the president to give them authority.

But if it shall appear that the decree has been promulgated on the proposition of the secretary of the department, the latter shall be responsible conjointly with the president.

ART. IV. The secretaryship of foreign affairs will be divided into three bureaus, one of diplomacy, another of navy, and another of commerce.

The first bureau will study and dispose of all questions pertaining to management of diplomatic negotiations with other powers and the correspondence of the government with them; the second will study all questions relating to the formation and organization of our navy, and the fitting out of such expeditions as the necessities of the revolution may require; and the third will have charge of everything relating to the internal and external commerce and the preliminary work which may be necessary for making treaties of commerce with other nations.

ART. V. The secretaryship of war will be divided into two bureaus—one of war, properly speaking, and the other of public works.

The first bureau will be subdivided into four sections—one of campaigns, another of military justice, another of military administration, and another of military health.

The section of campaigns will have charge of the appointment and formation of the certificates of enlistment and service of all who serve in the revolutionary militia; of the direction of campaigns; the prepation of plans, works of fortification, and preparing reports of battles; of the study of military tactics for the army, and the organization of the general staff, artillery and cavalry; and finally, of the determination of all the other questions concerning the business of campaigns and military operations.

The section of military justice will have charge of everything relating to courts of war and military tribunals, the appointment of judges and counsel, and the determination of all questions of military justice. The section of military administration will be charged with the furnishing of food and other supplies necessary for the use of the army, and the section of military health will have charge of everything relating to the hygiene and healthfulness of the militia.

ART. VI. The other secretaryships will be divided into such bureaus as their branches may require, and each bureau will be subdivided into sections according to the nature and importance of the work it has to do.

ART. VII. The secretary will inspect and supervise all the work of his secretaryship, and will determine all questions with the president of the government.

At the head of each bureau will be a director, and in each section an officer provided with such number of assistants and clerks as may be specified.

ART. VIII. The president will appoint the secretaries of his own free choice, and in concert with them will appoint all the subordinate officials of each secretaryship.

In order that in the choice of persons it may be possible to avoid favoritism it must be fully understood that the good name of the country and the triumph of the revolution require the services of persons truly capable.

ART. IX. The secretaries may be present at the revolutionary congress, in order that they may make any motion in the name of the president, or may be interpellated publicly by any one of the representatives; but when the question which is the object of the motion shall be put to vote, or after the interpellation is ended, they shall leave and shall not take part in the vote.

ART. X. The president of the government is the personification of the Philippine people, and in accordance with this idea it shall not be possible to hold him responsible while he fills the office.

His term of office shall last until the revolution triumphs, unless under extraordinary circumstances he shall feel obliged to offer his resignation to congress, in which case congress will elect whomsoever it considers most fit.

CHAPTER II.—*Of the revolutionary congress.*

ART. XI. The revolutionary congress is the body of representatives of the provinces of the Philippine Archipelago, elected in the manner prescribed in the decrees of the 18th of the present month.

Nevertheless, if any province shall not be able as yet to elect representatives because the greater part of its towns shall have not yet been able to liberate themselves from Spanish domination, the government shall have power to appoint, as provisional representatives for this province, those persons who are most distinguished for high character and social position, in such numbers as are prescribed by the above-named decree; provided, always, that they are natives of the province which they represent, or have resided therein for a long time.

ART. XII. The representatives having met at the town which is the seat of the revolutionary government, and in the building which may be designated, will proceed to its preliminary labors, designating by plurality of votes a commission composed of five individuals charged with examining documents accrediting each representative, and another commission composed of three individuals, who will examine the documents which the five of the former commission exhibit.

ART. XIII. On the following day the above-named representatives will meet again, and the two commissions will read their respective reports concerning the legality of the said documents, deciding by an absolute majority of votes on the character of those which appear doubtful.

This business completed, it will proceed to designate, also by absolute majority, a president, a vice-president, and two secretaries, who shall be chosen from among the representatives, whereupon the congress shall be considered organized and shall notify the government of the result of the election.

ART. XIV. The place where congress deliberates is sacred and inviolable, and no armed force shall enter therein unless the president thereof shall ask therefor in order to establish internal order disturbed by those who can neither honor themselves nor its august functions.

ART. XV. The powers of congress are: To watch over the general interest of the Philippine people, and the carrying out of the revolutionary laws; to discuss and vote upon said laws; to discuss and approve, prior to their ratification, treaties and loans; to examine and approve the accounts presented annually by the secretary of finance, as well as extraordinary and other taxes which may hereafter be imposed.

ART. XVI. Congress shall also be consulted in all grave and important questions, the determination of which admit of delay or adjournment: but the president of the government shall have power to decide questions of urgent character, but in that case he shall give account by message to said body of the decision which he has adopted.

ART. XVII. Every representative shall have power to present to congress any project of law, and every secretary, on the order of the president of the government, shall have similar power.

ART. XVIII. The sessions of congress shall be public, and only in cases which require reserve shall it have power to hold a secret session.

ART. XIX. In the order of its deliberations, as well as in the internal government of the body, the instructions which shall be formulated by the congress itself shall be observed.

The president shall direct the deliberations and shall not vote except in case of a tie, when he shall have the casting vote.

ART. XX. The president of the government shall not have power to interrupt in any manner the meetings of congress nor embarrass its sessions.

ART. XXI. The congress shall designate a permanent commission of justice, which shall be presided over by the auxiliary vice-president or each of the secretaries, and shall be composed of those persons and seven members elected by plurality of votes from among the representatives. This commission shall judge on appeal the criminal cases tried by the provincial courts, and shall take cognizance of and have original jurisdiction in all cases against the secretaries of the government, the chiefs of provinces and towns, and the provincial judges.

ART. XXII. In the office of the secretary of congress shall be kept a book of honor, wherein shall be recorded special services rendered the country and considered as such by said body. Every Filipino, whether in the military or civil service, may petition congress for notation in said book, presenting duly accredited documents describing the service rendered by him on behalf of the country since the beginning of the present revolution. For extraordinary services which may be rendered hereafter the government will propose said notation, accompanying the proposal with the necessary documents justifying it.

ART. XXIII. The congress will also grant on the proposal of the government rewards in money, which can be given only once, to the families of those who were victims of their duty and patriotism as a result of extraordinary acts of heroism.

ART. XXIV. The acts of congress shall not take effect until the president of the government orders their fulfillment and execution. Whenever the said president shall be of the opinion that any act is unsuitable, or against public policy, or pernicious, he shall explain to congress the reasons against its execution, and if the latter shall insist on its passage, the president shall have power to oppose his veto under his most rigid responsibility.

CHAPTER III.— *Of military courts and justice.*

ART. XXV. When the chiefs of military detachments have notice that any soldier has committed or has perpetrated any act of those commonly considered as military crimes, he shall bring it to the knowledge of the commandant of the zone, who shall appoint a judge and a secretary, who shall begin suit in the form prescribed in the instructions dated the 20th of the present month. If the accused shall be of the grade of lieutenant or higher, the said commandant shall himself be the judge, and if the latter shall be the accused the senior commandant of the province shall name as judge an officer who holds a higher grade, unless the same senior commandant shall himself have brought the suit. The judge shall always be a field officer.

ART. XXVI. On the conclusion of the preliminary hearing the senior commandant shall designate three officers of equal or higher rank to the judge, and the military court shall consist of said officers, the judge, the councilor, and the president. The latter shall be the commandant of the zone if the accused be of the grade of lieutenant or higher. This court shall conduct the trial in the form customary in the provincial courts, but the judgment shall be appealable to the higher courts of war.

ART. XXVII. The superior court shall be composed of six members, who shall hold rank not less than brigadier-generals, and the judge-advocate. If the number of generals present in the capital of the revolutionary government shall not be sufficient, the deficiency shall be supplied by representatives designated and commissioned by congress. The president of the court shall be the general having the highest rank of all, and should there be more than one having equal rank, the president shall be elected from among them by absolute majority of votes.

ART. XXVIII. The superior court shall have jurisdiction in all cases affecting the higher commandants, the commandants of zones, and all officers of the rank of major and higher.

ART. XXIX. Commit military crimes: First, those who fail to grant the necessary protection to foreigners, both in their persons and property, and those who similarly fail to afford protection to hospitals and ambulances, including persons and effects which may be found in possession of one or the other, and those engaged in the service of the same, provided always they commit no hostile act; second, those who fail in the respect due to the lives, money, and jewels of enemies who lay down their arms, and of prisoners of war; third, Filipinos who place themselves in the service of the enemy, acting as spies or disclosing to them secrets of war and the plans of the revolutionary positions and fortifications, and those who present themselves under a flag of truce without justifying properly their office and their personality; and fourth, those who fail to recognize a flag of truce duly accredited in the form prescribed by international law.

Will commit also military crimes: Those who conspire against the unity of the revolutionists, provoking rivalry between chiefs, and forming divisions and armed bands; second, those who solicit contributions without authority of the government and misappropriate the public funds; third, those who desert to the enemy, or are guilty of cowardice in the presence of the enemy, being armed; and fourth, those who seize the property of any person who has done no harm to the revolution, violate women, and assassinate or inflict serious wounds on unarmed persons, and who commit robberies and arson.

ART. XXX. Those who commit the crimes enumerated will be considered as declared enemies of the revolution, and will incur the penalties prescribed in the Spanish Penal Code, and in the highest grade.

If the crime shall not be found in the said code the offender shall be imprisoned until the revolution triumphs, unless the result of this shall be an irreparable damage, which, in the judgment of the tribunal, shall be a sufficient cause for imposing the penalty of death.

ADDITIONAL CLAUSES.

The government will establish abroad a revolutionary committee composed of a number, not yet determined, of persons most competent in the Philippine Archipelago. This committee will be divided into three delegations—one of diplomacy, another of the navy, and another of the army.

The delegation of diplomacy will arrange and conduct negotiations with foreign cabinets with a view to the recognition of the belligerency and independence of the Philippines.

The delegation of the navy will be charged with the studying and organizing of the Philippine navy, and preparing the expenditures which the necessities of the revolution may require.

The delegation of the army will study military tactics and the best form of organization for the general staff, artillery, and engineers, and whatever else may be necessary in order to fit out the Philippine army under the conditions required by modern progress.

ART. XXXII. The government will issue the necessary instructions for the proper execution of the present decree.

ART. XXXIII. All the decrees of the dictatorial government in conflict with the foregoing are hereby annulled.

Given at Cavite the 23d of June, 1898.

EMILIO AGUINALDO.

E.

[Original filed 1200–9 Philippine Insurgent Records.]

[Translation.]

1898.

Province of Batangas, town of Balayan.

ACT OF POPULAR ELECTIONS.

In the town of Balayan, province of Batangas, having been previously summoned, there assembled on July 3, 1898, all the citizens most conspicuous for their education, social position, and honorable conduct, from the center of the town as well as from the barrios, having been called to constitute the mass meeting provided by article 2 of the decree of the dictatorial government of the Philippines, dated June 18, 1898, said decree having been brought to this province by Mr. Santiago Rillo de León, with instructions to proceed to the election, by majority vote, of the presidente of the town and of a head (cabeza) for each barrio, as well as a commissioner of police and internal order, a commissioner of justice and civil registration, and a commissioner of revenue and of property, as set forth in article 3 of same decree.

Mr. Lorenzo Fenoy presided, delegated by Don Miguel Malvar, commissioned to establish civil organization in the towns already free from Spanish control. After having read aloud, both in Spanish and Tagalo, that clause of the decree ordering the election, as well as paragraph 2 of rule 38 of instructions of June 20, 1898, they proceeded with the balloting as directed, the following persons being elected.

(The names of men elected as heads of centro and barrios, and as commissioners of the town, follow here, and are omitted in translation.)

With the foregoing the proceedings terminated and, having drawn up the present act in duplicate, it was signed by the presidente with all those who had taken part in the mass meeting, the former retaining a copy of the same, the other remaining in possession of the present municipal mayor of the town for safe-keeping and delivery to the presidente (jefe) on the day which may be indicated by the dictatorial government.

Balayan, July 3, 1898.

(Omission is here made of the signatures of the members present at the mass meeting.)

DECREE.

BACOOR, *August 8, 1898.*

In view of the act of the constitution of the local board of the town of Balayan (Batangas), and considering that no comment nor protest has been presented against the same, I hereby decree the following: Said act is approved and confirmed in all its parts, so that the persons elected may discharge their respective duties in compliance with the provisions of the decree of June 18 and instructions of June 20, 1898.

Publish and announce this decree.

The president of the revolutionary government,

EMILIO AGUINALDO.

The secretary of the interior:

LEANDRO IBARRA.

F.

[Original filed 1200-6 Philippine Insurgent Records.]

RECORD CONCERNING THE ELECTION OF REPRESENTATIVES FROM PANGASINAN AND MEMBERS OF THE PROVINCIAL COUNCIL OF SAME.

REVOLUTIONARY GOVERNMENT OF THE PHILIPPINES.

I authorize in due form Don Severino de las Alas, director of the office of the department of the interior of this government, as my representative to preside at the election by majority vote of the members of council and the representatives of the province of Pangasinan, on the day when the local chiefs of the towns, after being sworn and taking possession of their offices, shall assemble for the above purpose in this government.

God keep you many years.

Malolos, September 27, 1898.

The President,

EMILIO AGUINALDO.

Mr. SEVERINO DE LAS ALAS,
  Director of the Office of the Department of the Interior.

In the town of Malolos, province of Bulacan, there assembled in the building of the department of the interior on September 27, 1898, having been summoned for that purpose, the presidentes of the towns of Lingayen, Santa Maria, Mangaldan, Binmaley, Urdaneta, Malasiqui, Sual, S. Jacinto, Aguilar, Pozorubio, Binalonan, Calasiao, Salasa, S. Manuel, Mangataren, San Fabian, Dagupan, Bayambang, Alcala, Villasis, Urbiztondo, Tayug, S. Isidro, Alara, and Asingan, of the province of Pangasinan, under the presidency of Mr. Severino de las Alas, special representative of the president of the revolutionary government, delegated to preside at the election of the civil governor of said province and councillors of police and internal order, of justice and civil registration, of revenue and property, and two representatives of the above province for congress, according to the decree of June 18th and instructions of June 20, 1898, and to this end they proceeded to choose a secretary and two examiners, the vote resulting in the election of Mr. Baldomero Alvear, Mr. Juan Galvan, and Mr. Catalino J. Palisoc, respectively, for the said offices.

This act concluded, they proceeded likewise to the election of the provincial governor and the councillors above mentioned, the result being as follows: For governor, Mr. Juan Quesada, by 15 votes; for councillor of police and internal order, Mr. Felipe Tango, 18 votes; for councillor of justice and civil registration, Mr. Juan Vengson, 10 votes; councillor of revenue and property, Mr. Rafael Tison, 15 votes, and as representatives, Mr. Vicente del Prado, 25 votes, and Mr. Antonio Feliciano, 22 votes.

And the president having invited those present to make any remarks upon or present any objection to the said election or the persons elected to such offices, the members stated that they had nothing to oppose to the same and were agreed upon the persons elected.

With the above the act was concluded. The present record of the proceedings being drawn up, was signed by those present, together with the representative of the president, the examiners, and the secretary.

SEVERINO DE LAS ALAS,
  Representing the President.

(The names of those attending the convention (meeting) are here omitted.)

DECREE.

MALOLOS, *September 30, 1898.*

In view of the act of election of governor, councillors of police and internal order, of justice, civil registration and the poll, of revenues and property, and the election of two representatives for the province of Pangasinán; and

Whereas in said elections the requirements and formalities were observed as prescribed in the decree of June 18 and the instructions of June 20, 1898, and that no opposition has been made to same or challenge advanced,

By virtue of the authority vested in me I hereby approve the election in all its parts.

This decree to be published and distributed, so that due notice may be taken thereof.

The president:

EMILIO AGUINALDO.

The secretary of the interior,

SEVERINO DE LAS ALAS,
For the Secretary.

G.

JULY 16, 1898, TO OCTOBER 2, 1899.—BRIEFS OF DECREES OF THE PRESIDENT AND ORDERS AND INSTRUCTIONS OF THE SECRETARY OF THE INTERIOR RELATING TO THE INTERNAL GOVERNMENT.—ORIGINAL FILED IN INSURGENT RECORDS 0–13.

Bacoor, July 16, 1898.—Decree: In compliance with the proposal of the secretary of the interior, and acting in accordance with its powers, this government decrees that members of provincial councils and popular juntas shall pay a tax of one peso on their commissions.

Bacoor, July 16, 1898.—In order to carry out the provisions of the decree of June 18, 1898, the government hereby forbids the local presidentes and other functionaries from exercising the functions of their offices until they have received their appointments from this government.

Bacoor, July 19, 1898.—On account of the small number of natives who live in Cavite at present, and in order that that town may occupy the place in the organization of towns to which it is entitled, this revolutionary government, in accordance with the recommendation of the secretary of the interior, declares it a barrio of the pueblo of San Roque.

Bacoor, July 20, 1898.—A petition having been presented from the inhabitants of a certain town of the island of Marinduque, Mindoro Province, asking that on account of its distance from that island they be given a separate government, this petition is approved and the island of Marinduque is established as a separate province, and will elect the officials prescribed in the decree of June 18.

Bacoor, July 25, 1898.—A petition having been presented from the inhabitants of the town of Lubang, asking that on account of its distance from the capital town of Mindoro it be annexed to the province of Cavite, the petition is approved and the town of Lubang is made a part of the province of Cavite.

Bacoor, July 26, 1898.—Decree of president: The heads of provinces are to call upon the patriotism of all Filipino clergy in charge of parishes in towns which have submitted to the revolutionary government, urging them to impress upon their parishioners, both from the pulpit and in the confessional, that in order that our independence should be secured it is necessary to give absolute adhesion to the revolutionary government and its worthy president, Don Emilio Aguinaldo. The secretary of the interior is to inform them that they can collect the tithes and allowances prescribed in the regulations of the Archbishop Santa Justa y Rufina.

Bacoor, July 27, 1898.—Letter of secretary of interior: The organization of towns prescribed in the decree of June 18, 1898, will be put into effect by special commissioners appointed for that purpose and not before they arrive.

Bacoor, August 10, 1898.—Decree of president: It being of the utmost necessity to establish provincial councils and local juntas in the towns and provinces of Northern Luzon, the powers conferred upon the president by article 7 of the decree of June 18, and article 3 of that of July 15, 1898, are delegated to Daniel Tirona, commander of the military expedition which is about to operate in that portion of this island.

Bacoor, August 12, 1898.—Letter of secretary of interior: The government desires to leave the question of the church untouched. Congress will meet shortly. It will decide upon questions of tithes and allowances to ecclesiastics.

Bacoor, August 13, 1898.—Letter of secretary of interior: A priest has been elected head of the ecclesiastics in the province of Nueva Ecija to protect their rights and interests. His election is approved.

Bacoor, August 15, 1898.—The military chief of the town of Alfonso, Cavite, having presented a petition for the annexation of a certain tract of land known as Kaylaway, of the jurisdiction of Nasugbu, Batangas, the secretary of the interior, after a careful study of the subject, gives his opinion against said annexation.

Bacoor, August 16, 1898.—Cock fighting, card playing, and other games will not be allowed to young boys and lads, who must expend their moment of leisure in corporal exercises, like racing, swimming, drilling, boxing, etc., for the development of their body and strength.

Bacoor, August 22, 1898.—Ordering that preparation be made for the transfer of the headquarters of the government to the town of Malolos, Bulacan.

Bacoor, August 22, 1898.—In answer to questions propounded by the local presidente of Baliwag, Bulacan, the secretary of the interior says that a fee of 50 cents can be charged to the parties concerned for each of the three public announcements of their marriage, and another of 1 peso and 50 cents for the recording of the marriage act. Civil marriage is always compulsory according to the views of our laws; canonical marriage can be celebrated if desired by parties. The fees to be collected will be in accordance with the regulations of Archbishop Santa Justa y Rufina.

Bacoor, August 22, 1898.—Informs the president of Malibay that the persons wishing to be married by the church may appear before the parish priest and ask him to perform the ceremony.

Bacoor, August 22, 1898.—According to regulations, fees to be charged for recording the birth or death of persons will be 20 cents. Church fees will be regulated by rules promulgated by Archbishop Santa Justa y Rufina.

Bacoor, August 25, 1898.—Letter of secretary of interior to governors of provinces: As the rumor which is spread about that the North Americans are going to take advantage of us injures our cause, as our friendly relations with them could not be more satisfactory, local presidentes are to see to it that such reports are stopped.

Bacoor, August 26, 1898.—Decree of president: Local presidentes to forward at once through provincial commanders the funds they have collected for the government.

Bacoor, August 26, 1898.—Order of secretary of the interior: Permission given to open a drug store in Indan, Cavite Province.

Bacoor, August 26, 1898.—Letter of secretary of interior stating that president has directed the secretary of the treasury to issue a circular concerning the value of copper coins.

Bacoor, August 26, 1898.—Decree of president approves provisionally organization of two barrios in Tayabas province into pueblos.

Bacoor, August 26, 1898.—Decree of president, repealing the one of August 26, 1898, which assigned the value of 2 and 4 cuartos to coins of 1 centimo and 2 centimos.

Bacoor, August 27, 1898.—Secretary of the interior, Leandro Ibarra, approves the petition of the inhabitants of Kalumpang, a barrio of Similoan, La Laguna, for their separation from the latter and their being recognized to establish their own town government and elect their officials.

Bacoor, August 29, 1898.—Letter of secretary of interior to governors of provinces: The elementary schools which have been abandoned are to be immediately reestablished, the instructors during the late Spanish régime to be preferred; the regulations for same in force under the Spanish Government to be continued for the time being. The town councils will watch over and inspect the schools.

Bacoor, September 1, 1898.—Letter of secretary of interior to governors of provinces: Civil authorities to use the utmost care to avoid conflicts with the clergy (native clergy—T.). Decree of July 26 to be rigidly complied with.

Bacoor, September 2, 1898.—Decree of president: The government in answer to the representations made by the commissioner for the establishment of popular government in Tayabas Province orders that Lucena be the capital of that province henceforth, in place of Tayabas.

Bacoor, September 2, 1898.—Decree of president: Appoints a governor of Tayabas Province, to hold office until elections for said post have been held.

Bacoor, September 3, 1898.—Decree of president: In reply to request of officer commanding in Pampanga Province the following is decreed. All property, real and personal, movable and immovable, including money and jewels taken from the enemy as booty of war, will be administered by the military authorities, and not by the local presidentes of the towns. They will turn them over to the military officials, forwarding an inventory to the secretary. Towns will have to supply food for troops in transit through them or quartered in them, charging the amount against the provincial military administration or the provincial treasury. Half fares will be paid for transportation of soldiers by railroad. An estimate of cost of establishing arsenal workshops to be made.

Malolos, September 9, 1898.—The director of the interior urges the secretary of the treasury to take steps to procure that subsidiary copper currency has the same value everywhere.

Malolos, September 12, 1898.—Letter of the secretary of the interior, ordering that nominations be submitted to the provincial governments of medical men to serve as civil medical officers of the provinces. Their orders covering sanitary matters will be obeyed.

Malolos, September 13, 1898.—Decree of president: Forbids dead bodies being carried uncoffined or in open coffins.

Malolos, September 14, 1898.—Decree of president: Assigns quarters for the use of the offices of the secretaries of war, interior, and treasury.

Malolos, September 17, 1898.—Decree of president: Provides methods by which young persons who desire to marry and whose parents refuse their consent can do so.

Malolos, September 19, 1898.—Decree of president: In accordance with request of the people there, changes the name of a town in Tayabas Province to Aguinaldo.

Malolos, September 23, 1898.—Letter of secretary of interior to presidents (governors) of provinces: Orders that the men who are going about collecting contributions of war without authorization are to be arrested and punished.

Malolos, September 24, 1898.—Letter of secretary of interior, giving instructions for the movement of the market in that town, prescribing what is to be done by the contractor to see that it is kept in a sanitary condition.

Malolos, October 7, 1898.—Letter of secretary of interior to the provincial governor of Batangas, stating that the local presidentes can collect the same fees as notaries when they act in their place.

Malolos, September 24, 1898.—Decree of president appointing the governor of Zambales to approve the result of elections held in that province and to receive the oaths of functionaries there to the new government.

Malolos, September 24, 1898.—Decree of president: The local presidentes are to act provisionally as notaries, drawing up and certifying to contracts and other acts; the commissioners of justice (delegados) will be present as witnesses. Public documents will be authenticated by the local presidentes. Provides for the execution of the Spanish law of 1889 upon legal documents by the local presidentes and commissioners of justice. Spanish stamped paper surcharged will be employed provisionally for documents for which stamped paper is prescribed.

Malolos, September 28, 1898.—Decree of president: In order to meet the necessities of government, the president increases the number of secretaries to six. The members of his counsel will be the secretaries of foreign affairs, war, interior, fomento, justice, treasury. The decree continues by appointing bureaus under the secretaryships, and prescribes the duties which will be assigned to them.

Malolos, October 1, 1898.—Letter of secretary of Interior to governors of provinces: Orders that lists of the police in every town are to be forwarded to him, so that the secretary of war may provide arms for them.

Malolos, October 3, 1898.—Decree of president: Tax on commissions to be $10 for that of a head of a province, $9 for presidentes of capitals of provinces, $8 for members of provincial councils, etc.

Malolos, October 4, 1898.—Decree of president: Henceforth the office of the secretary of foreign affairs will be composed of three bureaus—diplomacy, marine, and commerce.

Malolos, October 6, 1898.—Decree of president: As the decree of June 18, 1898, did not provide for a means of filling the vacancies which occur among civil officials, this decree prescribes methods to be followed in such cases.

Malolos, October 19, 1898.—Decree of president: So far the soldiers of the army have suffered more than they would in campaign. They have been badly lodged and worse fed. Directions to be sent to the heads of towns to see that soldiers quartered there are to be well lodged and well fed.

Malolos, October 20, 1898.—Letter of secretary of interior: The president has authorized the selection of a "Capitan de Sangleys" (head of the Chinese half-breeds) for certain towns in Manila Province. His duties will for the present be confined to collecting taxes from his people. The other attributes of his position will for the time be in abeyance.

Malolos, October 20, 1898.—Decree of president: Parish priests forbidden to sell wax candles. Priests nominated by the Archbishop of Manila will not be recognized unless approved by this government.

Malolos, October 26, 1898.—Decree of president: The church-building funds are to be strictly applied to the purposes for which they were intended. The secretary of the interior will provide for this.

Malolos, October 26, 1898.—Proclamation of president: States that his government has no desire to exercise authority within the limits of Manila occupied by the Americans. Persons who make arrests, search houses, and commit acts such as he permits only within his own jurisdiction will be declared outlaws, and brought before the courts-martial appointed by the revolutionary government.

Malolos, October 10, 1898.—Decree of president: Grants the request of people of certain barrios of the pueblo of Nagcarlan, Laguna Province, that they be declared separate pueblo. Appoints the provincial governor to carry out the provisions of this decree.

Malolos, November 2, 1898.—Decree of president: Declares all rules and regulations established by the Spanish Government upon hygiene and sanitary matters to be provisionally in force.

Malolos, November 3, 1898.—President Aguinaldo applies the provisions of the decree of June 11 to the question propounded by Mr. Paciano Mercado Rizal, of Calamba, Laguna, as to the title of property in that town.

Bacoor, August 22, 1898.—Decree of president: In view of the exceptional conditions in Manila he appoints a committee and subcommittee, charged with propaganda there; these committees and subcommittees to collect the taxes established there by the government and to carry out the other duties prescribed for them. Members of these committees must be upright Filipinos, devoted to the independence of the Philippines.

Bacoor, August 29, 1898.—Decree of president: He appoints the members of the directing committee of the committee in Manila; decrees of August 29 and September 2 on same matter.

(Note.—These series of original entries is preserved. It is probable that these decrees were issued in November and dated back.—T.)

Malolos, November 5, 1898.—Decree of president: Puts in effect the Spanish law of 1894 upon medical men attached to the provincial governments. Assigns stations to these of the various classes. Prescribes documents to be submitted by applicants for these positions. All of the provinces of Luzon will have these medical officials and some of the other islands.

Malolos, November 5, 1898.—Proclamation of the president: Prescribes measures to be taken providing against further escapes of prisoners of war.

Malolos, November 7, 1898.—Decree of president: Prescribes that 1 per cent of value of real property be charged for entering descriptions of estates in the registry of property.

Malolos, November 11, 1898.—Decree of president: Giving his decision against the petition of the inhabitants of Paete, Laguna, who want the town to be called, "Rizal."

Malolos, November 12, 1898.—Decree of president: Provides for assistants to the heads of barrios and pueblos.

Malolos, November 16, 1898.—Secretary of the interior to the president of the revolutionary congress: Requests him to report weekly the names of members who have been present at the sessions, and the excuses given by those who have been absent.

Malolos, November 16, 1898.—Decree of president: Calling upon presidentes of the towns of the province of Pampanga to use all their efforts to see that the national loan is subscribed for.

Malolos, November 16, 1898.—Letter of secretary of interior: Calling on the governors (heads) of provinces to check abuses which are being committed by certain officials.

Malolos, November 23, 1898.—Letter of instruction of the secretary of the interior to the governors of provinces: In order to provide for the local presidentes and other officials carrying out the laws and regulations prescribing their duties, the heads of provinces, or persons delegated by them, will inspect the accounts of the towns and their records. If any deficit or embezzlement is detected the official will be suspended and a new election held. Reports will be made of such cases, so that the offenders may be brought to trial. In this tour of inspection efforts must be made to induce the people to live in harmony. Reports to be made whether the towns are well administered.

Malolos, November 25, 1898.—Decree of president, providing for the creation of a bureau of census and statistics in the office of the secretary of the interior.

Malolos, December 1, 1898.—Secretary of interior appoints a commissioner to interrogate the friars, prisoners in Tarlac Province, and find out from them who broke into the parish house the day the province surrendered and what was carried off from it.

Malolos, December 5, 1898.—Secretary of interior informs the governors of the provinces that from that date all public documents and petitions must be on stamped paper of the value of 25 centimos a sheet.

Malolos, December 9, 1898.—Secretary of interior informs the governors of Tarlac, Pangasinán, Unión, Ilocos (Norte and Sur), Padre Burgos (Benguet), and Nueva Viscaya that people must not be disturbed in the exercise of their religion.

Malolos, December 12, 1898.—Decree of president: Appoints a lawyer to carry out certain investigations of offenses committed in Tarlac.

Malolos, December 23, 1898.—Decree of president: He is about to go to Cavite Viejo for a few days and authorizes the secretary of the interior to act upon routine matters of the latter's office without consulting him. Important matters will be held until his return.

Malolos, December 25, 1898.—Secretary of interior: Orders that the method of inspection of cattle before butchering employed under the Spanish Government be continued in force. Same fees to be collected.

Malolos, December 22, 1898.—Secretary of interior: In order to avoid the future commission of crimes in Zambales by people proceeding from other provinces, the governors of Pangasinán, Tarlac, Bataan, and Pampanga provinces are forbidden to let people enter Zambales without having passes issued by the heads of their towns stating who the bearer is and where he is going.

Malolos, December 29, 1898.—Secretary of interior appoints a commissioner to receive oaths of functionaries in Abra Province.

Malolos, January 2, 1899.—Decree of president: Authorizes the organization of a force of police in Nueva Ecija Province.

Malolos, December 23, 1898.—Decree of president: Appoints a Christian Chinaman in Tayabas Province to govern the Chinese there in the name of the revolutionary government.

Malolos, January 4, 1899.—Secretary of interior: Orders Malolos to be cleaned and preparations made for reception of a large number o people.

Malolos, January 5, 1899.—Decree of president: Suppresses the obligatory fifteen days of labor for the public service. In future all labor required for public purposes will be paid for. In case the country calls for the labor of her children, all will be called on to render it alike.

Malolos, January 7, 1899.—Secretary of interior: A bureau of census and statistics having been established, all governors of provinces are called upon to forward lists of people and animals in the towns under their jurisdiction.

Malolos, January 13, 1899.—Decree of president: Appoints a commissioner to establish committees in Tarlac Province to investigate the reforms needed for the progress of the country.

Malolos, January 16, 1899.—Decree of president: Appoints commissioner to hold elections in the island of Bohol, organizing there the government prescrbed in the decree of June 18, 1898, one of the commissioners to act temporarily as governor of the province.

Malolos, January 21, 1899.—Proclamation of Aguinaldo: Announces that on January 23, 1899, the president will take the oath of office.

Malolos, January 2, 1899.—Decree of president accepting the resignation of his cabinet on account of the reform in the constitution of his government. A. Mabini has formed a new cabinet, the members of which have been appointed by the president.

(NOTE.—The constitution of the Philippine republic went into effect January 23, 1899.)

Malolos, January 23, 1899.—Decree of president: Prescribes relations with foreigners. The tax provided for in the decree of November 30 will no longer be collected. As long as the independence of the Philippines is not officially recognized, all foreigners who desire to carry on any trade or profession in the territory of the republic will make a formal application to the secretary of fomento for permission to do so. This application will be accompanied by certificates from their consuls as to the applicant's nationality and occupation. Foreigners living remote from the capital will make the application to the head of the province in which they live. Foreigners provided with licenses are allowed to pass freely in the domain of the republic.

Malolos, January 23, 1899.—Decree of president: In order to celebrate the proclamation of the republic, all Spanish prisoners who do not belong to the regular army and all those who are suffering from illness of long duration will be liberated. The real property belonging to these Spaniards, as well as all property belonging to members of the Spanish regular army, will be kept until a convention in regard to this matter is agreed upon. All regular Spanish clergy, even those who are ecclesiastical dignitaries, and also the persons who, although they are not in holy orders, are yet connected permanently with said clergy, will be expelled from the Philippine territory. The government will appoint a permanent commission to investigate questions arising concerning the matter and to see that the exemptions established in the rules of warfare among the most civilized people are rigorously complied with. The papers giving the records of the embargoes carried out upon the property of Spaniards, who have not been prisoners of war, and Filipinos, will be submitted to this commission, who will decide whether these embargoes will stand.

(NOTE.—This decree was not carried out.—T.)

Malolos, January 25, 1899.—A. Mabini, president of the cabinet, appoints Wednesday and Saturday of each week as the days for holding sessions of the cabinet.

Malolos, January 25, 1899.—Decree of president: Governor of Pangasinan Province is appointed to receive the oaths of the civil functionaries among the Igarrotes there.

Malolos, January 25, 1899.—Decree of president: Appoints commissioner to establish in Samar the government provided for by the decree of June 18, 1898.

Malolos, January 28, 1899.—Secretary of interior appoints a commissioner to investigate the outrages committed on the head of Tambobo (Manila) by a captain of the Philippine army.

Malolos, January 28, 1899.—Secretary of interior: Orders towns to be cleaned, and measures of police to be taken; schools to be well kept up. Desires to show strangers in the country that the Filipinos know what is customary among civilized people.

Malolos, January 26, 1899.—Secretary of interior to governors of provinces: Orders that no payment of pensions to the families of men killed in campaign will be made without previous authorization by him.

Malolos, January 26, 1899.—Decree of the president: In view of the possibility of a war with the Americans, all fields will be planted so as to afford food for the people, great care to be taken to avoid having domestic animals injure the newly sown fields. Inspections to be made by heads of barrios to see that order is carried out.

Malolos, January 20, 1899.—Decree of the president: All military and civil officials and detachments of troops whose headquarters are more than 2 kilometers from a telegraph station will arrange for orderlies, whose sole duties will be to deliver telegrams to those officials. Provides also for delivery of telegrams addressed to private individuals; payment for latter to be made in telegraph stamps.

Malolos, February 11, 1899.—Decree of president: Appoints M. Trias secretary of treasury, civil and military commander in Cavite Province.

Malolos, February 13, 1899.—Decree of president: War having broken out with the Americans, provision is made for cooperation of the people in the defense of the Philippines. The local _juntas_ or municipal councils will serve as juntas of defense; these will appoint juntas of aid, whose duty will be to administer the money and material given by the people for the war; the junta of aid, with the assistance of the company of militia, which will be put by the local presidente at their disposal, will provide for lodging and feeding soldiers and guerillas who pass through the towns; they will tend the sick and wounded; they will provide for the maintenance of those detailed in the militia; they will provide all the supplies and assistance asked from the local presidente by the military administrator for regular soldiers and guerillas. The local presidentes will establish guards in the works of defense, will see that the people cultivate their fields, providing against a scarcity of food, and that those products are sold at a fair price. The local presidentes may grant licenses to bear firearms. Those who have arms under such license must fight for the defense of their towns or turn over their arms for this purpose when the necessity arises. The local presidentes will have the assimilated rank of commanders of guerillas, as prescribed in the general order of February 7.

Malolos, February 7, 1899.—General order of the president: Officers commanding zones and provinces are to encourage the troops who are cast down by the small advantages gained by the enemy. The old revolutionary leaders are called on; troops completely demoralized are to be disarmed. Those to whom arms are given must take oath not to use them for making assaults and other purposes prohibited by military honor. The leaders of bands will recognize no other leader than the commander of their zone or province, and will receive the necessary orders from him. They will act in conjunction with the regular forces, providing means of communication, unceasingly attacking and forming ambushes against the enemy. The military commanders of zones and provinces will report the bands which have been organized to the secretary of war, making complete returns, so that commissions may be sent to their commanders. The commanders of zones and of provinces will provide for the manufacture and reloading of cartridges.

Malolos, February 17, 1899.—Order of the secretary of the interior to governors of provinces: The juntas of defense will arrange for the immediate construction of trenches covering the roads over which the enemy may pass. In their construction the local juntas may employ the territorial militia organized according to the circular order of the secretary of the interior dated February 8, 1899. (Probably refers to preceding order.) This body will also supply guards for the trenches. Accounts are to be kept of the collections made by the juntas of aid; receipts will be given for amounts in specie received as a voluntary contribution from the people. These can be exchanged for bonds of the national loan. The juntas of aid will render accounts to the commissioners appointed by the government. In certain cases the juntas of aid will call for assistance upon the ladies of the Red Cross Association. Men not needed for the service will be kept at work in the fields. The moment any or all of the neighboring towns are invaded by the enemy the local presidente will put all men under arms who can be so used; half will be used for the defense of the menaced point and for support, the other half, under command of some thoroughly trustworthy person of the town, will act as reserve and place the property of the town, the old men, women, and children in a safe place. If there is a detachment of the regular army, or a band of guerillas in the town, the local presidente will make his dispositions in accordance with the commander of such force. Earnest efforts to be used to suppress bands of robbers. If persuasion will not serve, force must be used.

Malolos, February 28, 1899.—Secretary of the interior: Orders reports to be made by the governors of provinces, showing number of public buildings in the pueblos and the condition of same; condition of roads and bridges, what repairs are needed. In short, a general report upon the condition of the province.

Malolos, February 28, 1899.—Secretary of the interior: Order to governors of provinces forbidding use of corporal punishment.

Malolos, March 1, 1899.—Decree of the president: Repeats the order of the president issued February 4, 1899. All local presidentes are to place themselves at the orders of the military commanders of their province. He will not control them in their civil functions, but he will use their aid in the defense and preservation of the province. Military commanders will give receipts for all articles delivered to them. Provides for punishing local presidentes who do not obey. The provincial presidents (or governors) will, in case of invasion, use their efforts to assist the plans of the military commanders. When a province is invaded, the military commander can use the force of national militia and police of the towns, and the local presidentes, as chief commanders of those forces, will execute his orders. When the commanders need men for the regular force (army) at their orders, they will apply for them to the provincial presidents, who will immediately provide them, seeing that every town contributes its share in proportion to its population. Selection of recruits may be made by lot or by selection of the popular junta. Provides for punishment of those who fail to obey.

Malolos, March 7, 1899.—Secretary of interior: In reply to a request of the secretary of war calls on heads of provinces to call upon all ex-soldiers of the Spanish army to join the insurgent forces (refers to discharged native soldiers).

Malolos, February 23, 1899.—Decree of president: Certain barrios of the pueblo of Pila, Laguna Province, have applied to be combined as a new town. The local junta of Pila has recommended it, and the provincial government has approved. The new town is accordingly announced.

Malolos, March 6, 1899.—Decree of president: Constitutes in the same manner a new pueblo in Bulacan Province.

Malolos, March 15, 1899.—Secretary of the interior: Appoints a commissioner to inspect the conditions in northern Luzon. He is also given power to bring offenders to trial. Military and civil commanders to give him necessary aid and support.

Malolos, March 17, 1899.—Secretary of interior: Calls on governors of provinces to report whether the territorial militia is organized, and how many companies; how many policemen in each town; in what towns military detachments are stationed; names of towns on coast; distance between towns according to road taken by men on foot; waterways connecting towns; how many roads connecting province with adjoining ones. Maps of every province and each town therein to be submitted.

Malolos, March 20, 1899.—Secretary of interior forwards copies of " El Heraldo Filipino" containing the decree upon recruiting to the heads of provinces. These copies will be distributed to the local commanders of the province. The decree will be obeyed immediately. Brief of it follows.

Malolos, February 21, 1899.—Decree of president: The wise and prudent Spanish regulations upon recruiting are too slow in operation, hence, although they will be observed in times of peace, the government has suspended their operation and proclaims the following method to be employed in obtaining recruits for the army: As soon as the nation is at war the local presidentes, without waiting for further orders, will assemble all men between 18 and 19 and between 21 and 35 to draw lots for the number of conscripts needed. The presidentes of towns will submit a report according to the form herewith, showing the number of men available of these ages on January 1 each year. Those who are unfit to serve will be given an opportunity to state their case, and on May 15 each year the definite report will be forwarded to the provincial government. A copy will be filed in the town. Provides in what order classes of inhabitants will be drawn upon for recruits, unmarried men, married men without children, etc. When the drawing has taken place the conscripts will, if needed, be sent to the rendezvous of recruits; if not, they will remain in their pueblos, but must not leave them. Provides for exemption from service by payment. The women who are without support by the absence of men of the family in the ranks will be supported by the town. As the country is now at war, the conscription herein prescribed will be carried out as soon as these instructions are received. In order that all provinces shall contribute equally, the governors of provinces will report immediately to the secretary of war the number of men in their province subject to conscription. The secretary will designate the quota for each province. These methods will not be employed among non-Christian tribes. Their enlistment will be voluntary. In case there is not time to carry out these orders, there being urgent necessity to replace losses of men, the members of the local government will vote on the names of the men of the town of the proper ages, and those receiving the majority of votes will be sent as soldiers to the army.

Malolos, March 20, 1899.—Secretary of interior: Calls on governors of provinces to report names on hand in the juntas of aid.

Malolos, March 21, 1899.—Secretary of interior: Appoints a delegate to hold elections in Tarlac Province.

Malolos, March 21, 1899.—Secretary of interior: Orders governors of provinces to, as far as possible, train the men of their provinces so that they will be ready for service when they join the ranks, and to carry out their duty as territorial militia.

Malolos, March 21, 1899.—Decree of president: The governor of Ilocos Sur has consulted the government upon how to cover the deficiencies caused by the decree of January 5, 1899, abolishing compulsory labor. Will be covered by work of men who do not pay their taxes, or who are sentenced to hard labor. If necessary, call on the patriotism of the people, urging them to work for the public good.

Malolos, March 21, 1899.—Secretary of interior: Directs appointment of wardens for the public prisons provided for in the budget. To governors of provinces of Manila, Unión, Laguna, Ambos Camarines, Batangas, Bataan, Morong, Pampanga, Tayabas, Ilocos Norte, Ilocos Sur, Zambales, Albay, Mindoro, Sorsogon, Cavite, Tarlac, Neuva Ecija, Romblon, Cagayan, Abra, Isabela, Príncipe.

Malolos, March 24, 1899.—Secretary of interior to governors of provinces: Forbids gambling.

Malolos, March 24, 1899.—Decree of president: Appoints a commissioner to establish the revolutionary government in Paragua Island.

San Isidro, April 17, 1899.—Secretary of interior: The president of the cabinet directs him to inform governors of provinces that all persons who have paid the contribution of war ("certificates of citizenship"), will be respected in their persons and property, and will not be called upon for any public service without being paid therefor. They will not be required to obtain passes to go from one town to another. Those who have not taken out these papers will be employed in the civil and military public works. Provides penalties for infraction of this law.

San Isidro, April 22, 1899.—Secretary of interior: Appoints a commissioner to inspect conditions of Nueva Ecija, his traveling expenses to be met by local funds.

San Isidro, April 27, 1899.—Decree of president: Appoints Tomás Mascardo civil and military governor of a certain district in Pampanga.

San Isidro, April 28, 1899.—Decree of president: The federal council of the Visayas has been broken up by the majority of its members remaining in Iloilo, occupied by the American forces, and as it never had a representative character, never having had its members elected by the different islands which form the Visayas, the president of the republic, in accord with his cabinet, proclaims that the federal council of the Visayas is abolished as the government for Panay or the Visayas. In its place is established the provincial council of Iloilo, and Gen. Martin F. Delgado is appointed civil and military governor of that province. As military commander he will propose a second in command, and as a civil governor he will propose a secretary of the government. The latter is to be chosen from the people of the province. These men are authorized to carry out the functions of their offices provisionally until approved by the government. The secretary will be in charge of the branches of justice, police, and treasury, and will assist the governor. The second in command will assist the governor in the operations of war; in the absence of the governor he will replace him. The members of the council will be elected by a general junta of the most important persons of the province. Certified copies of the act of election will be sent to this government. Gen. Ananias Diocno is appointed military and civil governor of Capiz province. Gen. V. Lucban is appointed civil and military governor of the island of Samar. This decree will remain in force in the Visayas and elsewhere until the recognition of the independence of the archipelago. The general laws prevailing will obtain except where set aside by this decree.

San Isidro, April 29, 1899.—Decree of president: Appoints a commissioner to report upon complaints brought against civil officials in Nueva Vizcaya. If these are well founded he will hold new elections and bring the culprits to trial.

Cabanatúan, June 9, 1899.—Secretary of interior: Calls on governors of provinces to urge the presidentes of towns to induce the people to give horses and wagons for use of the troops. Those who do so will be given receipts and will be exempt from carrying baggage for and doing other personal service for the army.

Cabanatúan, June 8, 1899.—Secretary of interior to governors of provinces: The provisions of the constitution in regard to marriage will be exactly followed.

Cabanatúan, June 5, 1899.—Secretary of interior informs governors of provinces that the amounts to be paid for religious rites prescribed in the decree of Archbishop Santa Justa y Rufina will be collected. No distinction to be made, however, between mestizoes and Filipinos.

Tarlac, June 24, 1899.—Decree of president: States that in order to avoid parish funds in future being delivered to Archbishop Nozaleda (archbishop of Manila) by parish priests, as has been done, and as this is a highly unpatriotic act, Father Gregorio Aglipay is appointed a commissioner of the government to make a careful inspection of the parish funds of every town in Luzon. He will urge that they be invested in bonds of the national loan to avoid loss. He will draw up charges against those who oppose this. Civil and military officials will aid in every way.

Tarlac, June 26, 1899.—Secretary of interior has received confidential reports of the abuses committed by certain local presidentes in Pangasinán Province. Appoints a commissioner to investigate and bring charges against the guilty.

Tarlac, June 28, 1899.—Decree of president: In answer to the request of the governor of Pangasinán for a decision concerning the conflict between the Spanish laws declared in force by the constitution and the decree publishing the government estimates of receipts and expenses, the following decree upon cost of civil and canonical marriage is published: A marriage by a priest is to cost 12 reales (about 72 cents, gold), whereas a civil marriage will cost 3 pesos ($1.50, gold) for registering same.

Tarlac, July 3, 1899.—Decree of president: Pablo Ocampo is appointed the representative of this republic in Manila. He can appoint delegates if he considers it for the advantage of the republic, and will there carry out the instructions which will be given him. Before action upon matters of great importance he must obtain the previous sanction of this government.

Tarlac, July 4, 1899.—Decree of president: Upon application of certain barrios of Bayambang, in Pangasinán Province, to be constituted a separate town. An application approved by the governor of the province, they are constituted a town as requested.

Tarlac, July 7, 1899.—Decree of president: In order to duly celebrate the first anniversary of the proclamation of independence of the Philippines, a pardon is granted to all deserters from the army who within forty days surrender themselves and their arms. Certain classes of prisoners are also pardoned.

Tarlac, August 10, 1899.—Secretary of the interior: In order that parish funds and cash belonging to churches be removed from danger of loss by the hazards of war, they will all be invested in the national loan. Addressed to the governors of Southern Luzón and the provinces of Bataan, Zambales, Nueva Ecija, Pampanga, Bulacán, Morong, Tayabas, Laguna, Infanta, Cavite, Batangas, Mindoro Island, Romblon Island, Albay, Ambos Camarines, Sorsogón, Masbate Island,

Marinduque Island, Leyte Island, Samar Island, Bohol Island, Capiz, Iloilo, Antique (these three provinces form the island of Panay), and Cebú Island.

(NOTE.—This shows the extent of the jurisdiction exerted at that time.)

Tarlac, August 1, 1899.—Secretary of interior to the governors of Luzón: Directs them to forward to his office, so as to arrive by September 15, estimates of the receipts and expenditures of the towns in their provinces. These will clearly specify all the changes made in estimates of receipts and expenditures which they consider necessary. The greatest economy will be shown. This order is issued as the period for drawing up the yearly estimates in the towns and provinces has arrived, and the secretary of the interior desires to examine them and make the proper remarks upon the said estimates.

Tarlac, August 18, 1899.—Secretary of the interior to the governors of Luzón: Forwards model to be followed in drawing up lists of foreigners in the islands. Directions were published for the same in the "Gaceta de Filipinas," but the form was received too late for publication. It is now furnished.

Tarlac, August 21, 1899.—Secretary of the interior: Directs the governor of Nueva Ecija Province to have a presidente elected in San José to take the place of the one who has died.

Tarlac, August 22, 1899.—Secretary of the interior to governors of provinces: Calls their attention to the circular issued by the secretary of the treasury published in the "Gaceta de Filipinas" on the 13th of the present month. They are to use their utmost zeal in furnishing the data required for drawing up the estimates to be used in those of the nation for 1900. The number of police required in the towns must be estimated for; estimates to be made for transportation of recruits and money for the maintenance of prisoners, for the extermination of locusts, for public receptions and festivities, for the construction of public buildings and roads and for tools for same, for expenses of travel of medical men employed to vaccinate, for medicines for prisoners and the poor, for religious solemnities, and for rent of public buildings. At the proper time statements of the resources of the towns are to be rendered. Estimates in triplicate covering matters within the jurisdiction of the secretary of the interior will be furnished him. This circular is in amplification of the one of the 1st of the present month.

Tarlac, September 6, 1899.—Secretary of the interior calls on the governors of provinces to urge the parish priests, who are heralds of a religion of peace and charity, to support the government in the campaign it is waging against enemies of order. The secretary of war also joins in urging that the priests urge the people of evil life who are disturbing public tranquillity, perpetrating crimes of all kinds, injuring commerce and agriculture, to return to a life of industry. This is especially important now, that it behooves us to show to the world our cultivation and probity. Copies of this to be sent to all parish priests.

Tarlac, August 24, 1899.—Decree of president. The secretary of the interior forwards to governors of provinces the "Gaceta de Filipinas" of September 15, 1899, containing the decree of the president of the above date. It provides that couriers and postmasters are to be assimilated in rank to the members of the regular army.

Tarlac, October 2, 1899.—Secretary of interior to governors of provinces. Rules that the governors of provinces are the commanders of the police of their provinces, and will make appointment to the same on nominations of the presidentes of the pueblos to which they belong.

TARLAC, *September 6, 1899.*

H.

[Original filed No. 206-3 Philippine Insurgent Records.]

Emilio Aguinaldo y Famy, president of the revolutionary government of the Philippines and general-in-chief of the army.

This government, recognizing the necessity of having an organ which may announce to the civilized world and in particular to the Filipino people, not only its orders, but also the good news of the salvation and independence of the same, just as they believe and wish, I hereby decree the following:

ARTICLE 1. A newspaper is established which shall be called "El Heraldo de la Revolución Filipina," which shall be the property of the government.

ART. 2. The control and management of the paper shall be in the hands of the official in charge of the press bureau of the diplomatic office in the department of foreign relations, under the immediate inspection of the secretary and director of that branch.

ART. 3. The provisions which are inserted in said paper shall be of an official character.

ART. 4. All persons who wish to cooperate in the great undertaking of instructing the people in political life and to consolidate the union of all the Filipinos, whether they write either in the form of pamphlets or articles, may send in their work to said division in order that the publication may be made.

ART. 5. The paper shall be edited in the two languages, Tagalog and Spanish, so that all Filipinos may understand it. It shall be published once or twice a week, as circumstances may require.

ART. 6. The government may collect as subscriptions a moderate sum, which shall be used for the support of the press and the requirements of the revolution, if there should be any surplus.

ART. 7. Mr. Zacarias Fajardo is appointed to take charge of the printing and to be chief of the force. He shall keep a list of the people under his orders and shall distribute work in the proper manner.

ART. 8. While the abnormal conditions of the war continue any publication is prohibited without permission from the government.

Given in Cavite, July 4, 1898.

EMILIO AGUINALDO.

52.

GACETA DE FILIPINAS.

REPÚBLICA FILIPINA

Presidencia

Don Emilio Aguinaldo y Famy, Presidente de la República Filipina, Capitán General y en Jefe de su Ejército.

Con esta fecha vengo en decretar lo siguiente:

Artículo único. Se suprime el HERALDO FILIPINO y el ÍNDICE OFICIAL que le ha sustituido, creando en su lugar la GACETA DE FILIPINAS, para la publicación de las disposiciones del Gobierno, requisito necesario para que tengan caracter obligatorio, cuantas leyes y Decretos, etc. emanen del mismo.

Comuníquese y publíquese para general conocimiento.

Dado en Cabanatúan á quince de Mayo de mil ochocientos noventa y nueve.— El Presidente de la República, *Emilio Aguinaldo.*—El Presidente del Consejo de Gobierno, *Pedro A. Paterno.*

AL HONORABLE SR. D. PEDRO ALEJANDRO PATERNO.

Aceptada la dimisión del Consejo de Secretarios que bajo la Presidencia del Sr. D. Apolinario Mabini, venía desempeñándolos, hé tenido por conveniente, en uso de las facultades que me concede la Constitución del Estado, encargar á V. la formación del nuevo Gabinete de Gobierno.

Dios guarde á V. muchos años.—San Isidro 7 de Mayo de 1899.—El Presidente, *Emilio Aguinaldo.*—Hay un sello que dice:—"República Filipina.—Presidencia."

AL HONORABLE PRESIDENTE DEL CONSEJO DE SECRETARIOS DE GOBIERNO, D. PEDRO ALEJANDRO PATERNO.

Con esta fecha he tenido á bien aprobar la relación de Secretarios de Gobierno que se ha servido remitirme y es la siguiente:

Secretario de Relaciones Exteriores, D. Felipe Buencamino.

Secretario del Interior, D. Severino de las Alas y Móxica.

Secretario de Guerra y Marina, D. Mariano Trias.

REPÚBLICA FILIPINA

Presidencia

D. Emilio Aguinaldo at Famy, Presidente nang República Filipina, Capitán General at Pañgulo nğ caniyang Hocbó.

Nğayon ay iniuutos co ang casunod:

Tanging articulo. Iniáalis ang "Heraldo Filipino" at ang "Indice Oficial" na napalit sa caniya, at ang ihabalili ay "Gaceta de Filipinas" na paghahayagan nğ mğa pasiya nğ Gobierno, bagay na cailañgan upang maipilit ang alinmang leyes at Decretos etc. na ilagda niya.

Ipabatid at iháyag upang matanto nğ lahat.

Lagda sa Cabanatuan icalabinglima nğ Mayo nğ sanglibo ualong daan siam na puo't siam.—Ang Presidente nğ República, *Emilio Aguinaldo.*—Ang Presidente nğ Consejo nğ Gobierno, *Pedro A. Paterno.*

SA CAGALANGGALANG NA GUINOONG D. PEDRO ALEJANDRO PATERNO.

Nğ matangap ang pamimitiw nğ Consejo nang Secretarios na sa ilalim nğ Presidencia ni Guinoong D. Apolinario Mabini, na guinaganap noon, minarapat cong sa paggamit nğ capangyarihang caloob sa aquin nğ Constitución nğ Estado, ay ipagcatiuala sa Inyo ang pagbabañgon nğ bagong Gabinete nğ Gobierno.

Ingatan cayo nğ Dios nğ mahabang panahon.—San Isidro 7 nğ Mayo nğ 1899.—Ang Presidente, *Emilio Aguinaldo.*—May isang tactac na ang sulit ay: "República Filipina.—Presidencia."

SA CAGALANGGALANG NA PRESIDENTE NğGONSEJO NğSECRETARIOS NğGOBIERNO, D. PEDRO ALEJANDRO PATERNO.

Minagaling cong aprobahan ang relación nang Secretarios nğ Gobierno na minarapat ninyong ipadala sa aquin at ito'y ang sumusunod:

Secretario nğ Relaciones Exteriores, D. Felipe Buencamino.

Secretario nğ Interior, D. Séverino de las Alas y Móxica.

Secretario nğ Guerra y Marina, D. Mariano Trias.

I.

[Pages 76–78 of report of Maj.-Gen. E. S Otis, U. S. Volunteers, on Military Operations and Civil Affairs in the Philippine Islands.]

The government of the Philippines has considered it its duty to set forth to the civilized powers the facts determining the rupture of its amicable relations with the army of the United States of America in these islands, to the end that they may thereby reach the conviction that I, for my part, have done everything possible to avoid it, although at the cost of many rights uselessly sacrificed.

After the naval combat, which occurred on May 1, of last year, between the Spanish squadron and that of America, the commander of the latter consented to my return from Hongkong to this beloved soil, and he distributed among the Filipinos some rifles found in the arsenal at Cavite, doubtless with the intention of reestablishing the revolution, somewhat quieted by the convention of Biac-na-Bató, in order to have the Filipinos on his side.

The people, influenced by the declaration of war between the United States and Spain, understood the necessity of fighting for their liberty, feeling sure that Spain would be destroyed and rendered incapable of leading them along the road to prosperity and progress. The Filipinos hailed my advent with joy, and I had the honor of being proclaimed leader on account of the services which I had rendered in the former revolution.

Then all the Filipinos without distinction of classes took arms, and every province hastened to expel from its frontiers the Spanish forces. This is the explanation of the fact that, after the lapse of so short a period of time, my government rules the whole of Luzón, the Visayan Islands, and a part of Mindanao.

Although the North Americans took no part in these military operations, which cost no little blood and gold, my government does not disavow the fact that the destruction of the Spanish squadron and the gift of some rifles from the arsenal to my people influenced the progress of our arms to some extent. It was also taken for granted that the American forces would necessarily sympathize with the revolution which they had managed to encourage, and which had saved them much blood and great hardships; and above all, we entertained absolute confidence in the history and traditions of a people which fought for its independence and for the abolition of slavery, which posed as the champion liberator of oppressed peoples; we felt ourselves under the safeguard of a free people.

The Americans seeing the friendly disposition of the Filipino people, disembarked forces at the town of Parañaque and took up positions all along the line occupied by my troops, as far as Maytubig, taking possession of many trenches constructed by my people, by the employment of astuteness, not unaccompanied by violence. They forced a capitulation on the garrison of Manila, which, inasmuch as it was invested by my troops, was compelled to surrender at the first attack. In this I took a very active part, although I was not notified, my forces reaching as far as the suburbs of Malate, Ermita, Paco, Sampaloc, and Tondo.

Notwithstanding these services, and although the Spaniards would

not have surrendered but for the fact that my troops had closed every
avenue of escape to the towns of the interior, the American generals
not only ignored me entirely in the stipulations for capitulation, but
also requested that my forces should retire from the port of Cavite
and the suburbs of Manila.

I represented to the American generals the injustice done me, and
requested in friendly terms that they should at least expressly recognize my cooperation, but they utterly declined to do so. Nevertheless, being always desirous of showing friendliness and good feeling
toward those who call themselves liberators of the Philippine people,
I ordered my troops to evacuate the port of Cavite and the suburbs
of Ermita, Malate, Sampaloc, and Tondo, retaining only a portion of
the suburb of Paco.

In spite of these concessions, not many days passed before Admiral
Dewey, without any reason whatever, arrested our steam launches,
which had been plying in the bay of Manila with his express consent.
Almost at the same time I received a letter from General Otis, commander of the American army of occupation, demanding that I should
withdraw my forces beyond the lines marked on a map which he also
sent me, and which showed within the lines of the town of Pandacan
and the hamlet of Singalong, which never have belonged to the municipal area of Manila and its suburbs.

In view of this unjustifiable attitude of both American leaders, I
summoned a council of my generals, and asked the advice of my cabinet, and in conformity with the opinion of both bodies I named commissioners, who placed themselves in communication with these
Americans. Although Admiral Dewey received in an insolent manner
and with aggressive phrases my commissioners, whom he did not permit to speak, I yielded to the friendly suggestions of General Otis,
withdrawing my forces to the desired line for the purpose of avoiding
contact with his troops. This gave rise to many misunderstandings,
but I hoped that once the Paris conference was at an end my people
would obtain the independence promised them by the consul-general
in Singapore, Mr. Pratt, and that the friendship formerly assured and
proclaimed in manifestoes and speeches would be established by the
American generals who have reached these shores.

But it did not turn out thus. The said generals accepted my concessions in favor of peace and friendship as indications of weakness.
Thus it is, that with rising ambition, they ordered forces to Iloilo on
December 26, with the purpose of acquiring for themselves the title
of conquerors of that portion of the Philippine Islands occupied by
my government.

Such procedures, so foreign to the dictates of culture and the usages
observed by civilized nations, gave me the right to act without observ-
ing the usual rules of intercourse. Nevertheless, in order to be correct to the end, I sent to General Otis commissioners charged to solicit
him to desist from his rash enterprise, but they were not listened to.

My government can not remain indifferent in view of such a violent
and aggressive seizure of a portion of its territory by a nation which
has arrogated to itself the title, "champion of oppressed nations."
Thus it is that my government is ready to open hostilities if the American troops attempt to take forcible possession of the Visayan Islands.
I denounce these acts before the world, in order that the conscience of

55

mankind may pronounce its infallible verdict as to who are the true oppressors of nations and the tormentors of human kind.

Upon their heads be all the blood which may be shed.

EMILIO AGUINALDO.

MALOLOS, *January 5, 1899.*

NOTE.—Upon January 8, 1899, this proclamation was reissued with the following change in the last paragraph but one: "—— attempt to take forcible possession of any part of the territory submitted to its jurisdiction," in place of, "attempt to take forcible possession of the Visayan Islands."

In the original translation, printed in General Otis's report, "ready" in the last paragraph but one is translated "disposed," which is not right.

[Copied from page 95 of the report of Maj. Gen E S. Otis, U. S Volunteers, on military operations and civil affairs in the Philippine Islands, 1899]

GENERAL ORDER TO THE PHILIPPINE ARMY.

Nine o'clock p. m., this date, I received from Caloocan Station a message communicated to me that the American forces, without prior notification or any just motive, attacked our camp at San Juan del Monte, and our forces garrisoning the blockhouses around the outskirts of Manila, causing losses among our soldiers, who, in view of this unexpected aggression and of the decided attack of the aggressors, were obliged to defend themselves until the firing became general all along the line.

No one can deplore more than I this rupture of hostilities. I have a clear conscience that I have endeavored to avoid it at all costs, using all my efforts to preserve friendship with the army of occupation, even at the cost of not a few humiliations and many sacrificed rights.

But is is my unavoidable duty to maintain the integrity of the national honor and that of the army so unjustly attacked by those who, posing as our friends and liberators, attempted to dominate us in place of the Spaniards, as is shown by the grievances enumerated in my manifesto of January 8 last, such as the continued outrages and violent exactions committed against the people of Manila, the useless conferences, and all my frustrated efforts in favor of peace and concord.

Summoned by this unexpected provocation, urged by the duties imposed upon me by honor and patriotism and for the defense of the nation intrusted to me, calling on God as a witness of my good faith and the uprightness of my intentions, I order and command:

1. Peace and friendly relations between the Philippine forces and the American forces of occupation are broken, and the latter will be treated as enemies, with the limits prescribed by the laws of war.

2. American soldiers who may be captured by the Philippine forces will be treated as prisoners of war.

3. This proclamation shall be communicated to the accredited consuls of Manila and to congress, in order that it may accord the suspension of the constitutional guaranties and the resulting declaration of war.

Given at Malolos February 4, 1899.

EMILIO AGUINALDO,
General in Chief.

J.

From account books covering the period May 31, 1898, to September 2, 1899.

SOURCES OF REVENUE.

Taxes	$400,986.40
Seizures	361,668.50
Stamps	113,795.24
Hacienda taxes	17,179.15
Opium contracts	16,176.76
Cash seizures	70,276.48
Provincial taxes	3,914.89
Deposits under leases	13,855.72
Donations	76,093.96
Bonds of national loan	388,650.00
Suspense accounts	65,272.17
Titles and poll taxes	136,194.46
Remittances	459,200.78
Loans	143,771.08
General taxes, births, marriages, deaths, weights and measures, slaughter of cattle, etc	61,049.21
Forest products	621.45
Cargoes	10,443.01
Debts receivable	230,256.33
Repayments to treasury	17,327.89
	2,586,733.48

Balance September 2, 1899, last day on which accounts were kept 201,027.69

Statement of receipts of the Philippine revolutionary government, divided into provinces, May 31, 1898, to September 1, 1899.

Untraceable	$711,992.74	Isabela	$20,019.50
Pangasinán	204,448.02	Cavite	18,609.62
Cagayan	198,061.73	Morong	14,326.79
Albay	176,687.55	Mindoro	13,311.48
Unión	153,998.70	Masbate	11,243.17
Laguna	111,339.61	Bataan	9,236.81
Samar	106,466.01	Nueva Vizcaya	6,221.58
Manila	89,915.73	Panay	4,476.03
Bulacan	89,013.27	Abra	3,967.00
Leyte	87,719.74	Batanes Island	3,528.52
Batangas	74,058.18	Cebú	3,351.52
Ilocos Norte	73,192.03	Mindanao	3,108.10
Tarlac	58,625.76	Benguet	1,076.00
Nueva Ecija	51,196.06	Babuyanes Island	953.50
Ilocos Sur	51,669.21	Negros	834.00
Pampanga	51,051.71	Infanta	684.00
Tayabas	44,407.40	Lepanto	351.25
Sorsogon	39,251.00	Marinduque	198.00
Zambales	36,432.38		
Camarines	31,743.00		2,586,733.48
Romblon	29,966.78		

K.

Manila, Oct. 15, 1898 (816–1).—S. Mendezona, a merchant of Manila, writes to the president of the revolutionary government as representative of the firm of Mendezona & Co., of Manila, and applies for license to continue his trade in hemp (abacá) in Albay, Ambos Camarines, Sorsogón, Leyte, and Samar, where he has agents. States that his vessels will sail from Manila and Hongkong, and that he has given his personal adhesion to the government of Aguinaldo, and is ready to pay the taxes which it may require of him.

Malolos, Oct. 17, 1898 (42–7).—President decreed that all property for sale transported by river, railroad, or sea should pay 5 per cent of its value at point of shipment. Property exported from ports under control of his government to foreign ports are to pay 15 per cent of their value. Property imported from foreign ports is to pay 5 per cent ad valorem.

Malolos, Nov. 7, 1898 (1152–8).—Telegram of secretary of the treasury suspending the tax of 5 per cent on merchandise (probably that laid by decree of Oct. 17, 1898).

Malolos, Nov. 8, 1898 (1152–8).—Telegram of secretary of treasury. By order of president, article 1 of decree of Oct. 17, 1898, is reenforced. Telegram of yesterday of no effect.

Malolos, Nov. 15, 1898 (1152–8).—Telegram of secretary of treasury to civil governors and military commanders, by order of president, suspending collection of 5 per cent tax on merchandise shipped by land or water.

Legaspi, Albay Pvovince, Nov. and Dec., 1898 (258–2).—Protest of Smith, Bell & Co. against payment of duties on export of hemp (abacá) from that port to the insurgent government, on the ground that export duties will also be charged at Manila, and that the hemp was bought during the period when the province was in the hands of the Spanish Government. Protest is overruled by the secretary of the treasury of the insurgent government, who orders that the duties be not refunded to Smith, Bell & Co.

Malolos, Nov. 30, 1898 (1057–1).—Decree of president. This decree provided that foreigners were to pay from 100 to 5,000 pesos for license to carry on any business in the territory under control of the revolutionary government.

Tabaco, Albay Province, Dec. 1, 1898 (42–6).—General Vito Belarmino reports that he has collected the 5 per cent charged for pilotage and customs duties from four vessels—Elcano, Venus, Serafin, and Toyo-Morn; total amounting to 3,043.48 pesos, which will be turned over to the provincial treasury for account of the government.

Malolos, Dec. 8, 1898 (1152–8).—President of government to civil governors and military commanders of Batangas, Cavite, Laguna, Ambos Ilocos, Cagayán, Bulacán, Pangasinán, Tayabas, Ambos Camarines, Albay, Sorsogón, Unión, and Zambales (provinces): You are held responsible that no merchant vessel is allowed to enter the ports of your province without a pass from this government, except those coming directly from foreign ports.

Iloilo, Dec. 13, 1898 (733–1).—J. McMicking, agent of Warner, Barnes & Co., offers to forward letters from Aguinaldo to Negros Island; reports that Gen. Rios, Spanish governor-general, commanding at Iloilo, has forbidden communication with Guimaras Island, which makes communication with Negros more difficult.

Tabaco and Legaspi, Albay Province, Dec. 30, 1898 (42–8).—E. Aguinaldo informs his secretary of the treasury that the military commander of Albay Province informs him that he has turned into the provincial treasury since Dec. 11th, 1898, 7,405.41 pesos, received from customs duties.

Tacloban, Leyte, Jan. 5, 1899 (756–6).—V. Lucban, commanding in

Leyte and Samar, forwards to the president of the Philippine republíc
2,302.31 pesos, amount collected as customs duties, 5 per cent of value
of cargo collected from the vessel *Julia*, belonging to Smith, Bell & Co.

Legaspi, Albay, Jan. 18, 1899 (42–2).—S. H. Osmond, agent of
Smith, Bell & Co., ordered to pay duties on 2,601 pounds of abacá
exported.

Manila, Jan. 20, 1899 (238–2).—Smith, Bell & Co. protest to the
president of the revolutionary government in the Philippines against
the collection of certain duties, and ask for return of 4,328.55 pesos
paid by their agent at Tacloban to the insurgent customs officer there,
as 5 per cent on value of certain hemp (abacá). E. Aguinaldo in his
endorsement thereon rules that the provisions of his decree of Nov. 17,
1898, apply. Their protest is on the ground that export duties will
also be charged at Manila, and that they bought the hemp while the
province was in the hands of the Spanish Government.

Malolos, Jan. 23, 1899 (119–10).—Decree of the president: The
extraordinary contributions of war required by decree of Nov. 30
from foreigners and Spaniards desiring to carry on commerce or any
business in these islands is abolished; but all foreigners who desire to
carry on any business must first make an application for authority
therefor to the secretary de.fomento. This is to be accompanied by
a certificate of the consul of their country, in which he states their
nationality and profession. The desired authorization will then be
issued, if approved by the president of the republic. When the State
is declared in a state of war these authorizations will be issued by the
secretary of war and the military commanders of the provinces.
Freedom of movement will be permitted to persons thus authorized,
unless they commit offenses, which should be taken cognizance of by
tribunals of justice.

Manila, Jan. 25, 1899 (463–3).—John T. Macleod, manager of the
"Compañía Marítima," of Manila, applies to "the president of the
revolutionary government" at Malolos for five licenses for the steam-
ships *Unión, Salvadora, Brutus, España,* and *Elcano,* to engage in
coastwise trade between ports under control of the Philippine government. He forwards by bearer of letter 1,506.68 pesos, tonnage duties
on said vessels at 50 céntimos per ton.

Legaspi, Albay, Feb. 10, 1899 (42–1).—S. S. *Santander* and *Kongsee*
pay duties amounting to 6,588.10 pesos; port charges, 573.03 pesos.

Cabanatúan, February 25, 1899 (42–3).—Japanese ship "Hokoku-
Maru" pays $4,100 customs dues at that port, to be paid by Smith,
Bell & Co.'s agents at Cebú.

Albay, March 11, 1899 (258–1).—(Agent for Smith, Bell & Co.).
Pays duty of $2,759.60 on tobacco sent from Albay by steamship
"España."

Malolos, March 13, 1899 (42–9).—Telegram from A. Mabini, president of the council of government (cabinet), to the commander at
Aparri, informing him that in accordance with the law going into
effect April 1, 1899, no duties will be collected on imports or exports
by sea; that there will be a tax of 10 per cent for pilotage.

Samar, March 27, 1899 (221–4).—V. Lucban, general commanding
in Samar, forwards 80,761.85 pesos to secretary of the treasury in
drafts on Aldecoa & Co., merchants of Manila. This amount is
receipted for at Catbalogan by Francisco Enaje.

Legaspi, Albay, March 31, 1899 (42–3).—Secretary of war of insurgent government, in letter dated March 13, 1899, reports that he has received a letter from Gen. Vito Belarmino, dated March 31, 1899, in which he says: "I have the high honor to inform you that since the 15th of the present month no merchant vessel has anchored in this port of Legaspi, except the Japanese steamship 'Hokoku-Maru,' which anchored the afternoon of the 25th of the current month, coming from Cebú. Customs duties amounting to 3,200 pesos have been collected from her; for tonnage, 836.41 pesos, and for port duties, 83.64 pesos, making a total amount of 4,120.05 pesos. It will be paid by Mr. Walter Easton, representative of Smith, Bell & Co., merchants of Manila, as the consignees have no money on hand."

San Isidro, May 4, 1899 (105-10).—President Aguinaldo to the secretary of the treasury states that steamship "Hokoku-Maru" visited Legaspi, paying $4,120 customs dues through draft on Smith, Bell & Co., in Manilà.

Bayambang, Pangasinán, May 8, 1899 (258-5).—C. M. Clark, agent there of Smith, Bell & Co., in a letter addressed to the honorable President Don Emilio Aguinaldo, San Isidro, informs him that from Feb. 4, 1899, to date he has bought palay and rice to the value of 200,000 pesos on account of his firm, Smith, Bell & Co., and "the town of Bayambang can inform you that in the past events I have been somewhat of service to your cause."

Tarlac, July 1, 1899 (221-4).—Draft of letter from secretary of treasury to V. Lucban acknowledging receipt of 184,916.61 pesos— 104,973.01 pesos from Samar and 79,943.60 from Leyte—total amount in drafts issued in favor of Francisco Enaje, who brought the said sum.

Tarlac, July 24, 1899 (910-3).—Decree of president: No merchant vessel under the American flag will be admitted in the ports of the jurisdiction of this government. Vessels of other nationalities will be. No vessel will be permitted to discharge its cargo and passengers until it has been inspected by the military commander of the port. He will inspect the papers of the ship and he will certify to this. If the passenger is a foreigner he will report to the military commander of the port his nationality and the object of his journey, exhibiting to him the certificate of his consul as to his status. Copies of this decree are to be forwarded to the foreign consuls.

Tarlac, July 31, 1899 (119-7).—Decree of president, providing for registry of all foreigners. In order to be inscribed upon their register application must be made to the president, application to be accompanied by certificates of the consul of applicant, showing his nationality and occupation. In order to engage in business, permission must be obtained from the president of the republic.

Tarlac, Oct. 6, 1899 (266-2).—Permits exportation of products of the country except such as may be needed in the country on account of the scarcity of food among the poor, or which may be useful to the enemy. Authorization must first be obtained from the president of the republic, or from the governor or military commander of the province, in case it is distant from the seat of government.

Tarlac, Oct. 7, 1899 (1152-8).—Secretary of treasury to governor of Pangasinán: Delegates of towns and provincial officials charged with collecting taxes will collect tax on coastwise trade, which means from one port to another. Money collected will be paid into provincial treasury monthly.

Tarlac, Oct. 14, 1899 (1152–8).—Assistant secretary of navy to governor of Pangasinán: Duties will be imposed only on merchandise of coastwise trade, viz, upon vessels going from one province to another by water.

Laoag, Ilocos Norte, received at Tarlac Oct. 27, 1899 (190–6).—Telegram. General Tinio to the honorable president and captain-general, Tarlac: "I have the honor to inform you that my question was (in regard to following matter). The vessels which come here belong to foreign establishments not American, established in Manila. American laws do not permit engaging in coastwise trade without taking out papers, but in spite of that they do not enter with the American flag, but with a white one. Should we take possession of them also? I must inform you that all of them, including those of the Tabacalera (Compañía General de Tabacos), pay for papers, as they come from American jurisdiction. I ask for a prompt reply; as they are arriving rapidly, bringing articles of necessity for the province, and buying products of the same."

Laoag, Ilocos Norte, Oct. 31, 1899 (322–9).—M. Macias, superintendent in Ilocos Norte of the Compañia General de Tabacos de Filipinas, to M. C. Fermin, representative of Ilocos Norte in insurgent congress, asks him to use his influence with the president (E. Aguinaldo) to obtain the annulment of the embargo placed upon the tobacco property of said company, "using as an argument all that which you know the company has been doing for these provinces since October of last year." He also urges that permission be granted for vessels flying the American flag to enter the ports.

Ligao, Albay, April 18, 1900 (2006–1).—R. E. Santos, general military administrator, orders that all merchants, foreign and Philippine, dealing in hemp (abacá) must have permits from the insurgent government. Licenses to buy and sell hemp must be inspected by the local authorities, and must be procured also by those employed in transporting articles of various kinds, especially by those engaged in carrying hemp to the ports.

Albay Province, May 10, 1900 (733–2).—Correspondence between agents of Warner, Barnes & Co. and insurgents showing purchase of hemp from insurgents then in the field against the forces of the United States. Copy of translations attached as exhibit Ka. V. Belarmino, insurgent general, commanding in Albay Province.

Cebú, Oct. 29, 1900 (884–4).—P. Pardo, probably to V. Lucban, insurgent general, states that he is an employee of a foreign firm and is thinking of leaving it and setting up in business on his own account, continues: "Would you like to join me?—calling the firm, 'Enaje & Co.', although it would be carried on with the money of this government, as is done by some Philippine firms in Manila, who are trading with the money of Magdalo (E. Aguinaldo), P. García, Trias, and others, and these establishments pay their foreign accounts with the amounts received from the sale of their cargoes, and employ their profits in continuing the war. I need $10,000 in addition to my $10,000. Please reply to your devoted, P. Pardo."

Ka.

[Original filed No. 733–2 Philippine Insurgent Records.]

NOTES.

"*V. B.*"—Evidently the insurgent general Vito Belarmino. He commanded the district of Camarines, Albay, and Sorsogón.

Ramón Santos.—Was colonel in the insurgent army and adjutant-general to Belarmino.

Juan Acuña.—Confidential clerk to Colonel Ramón Santos, adjutant-general to General Vito Belarmino. At the time of this correspondence Vito Belarmino, Ramón Santos, and Juan Acuña were in active insurrection against the authority of the United States.

Albert E. Launders.—Agent for Warner, Barnes & Co., in Legaspi, Albay Province.

Arnaldo De Silvas, A. José Silvas, Legaspi.—Employee of Warner, Barnes & Co. One letter refers to him as bookkeeper.

---

(1) LIGAO, *May 10th, 1900.*
Messrs. WARNER, BARNES & COMPANY,
    Legaspi:

Upon the receipt of this you will cause to be paid to Mr. Luís Thomas the sum of $700.00, and charge the same to me.

Yours, etc.,
(Sgd.)   JUAN ACUÑA.

---

(2) LIGAO, *May 10th, 1900.*
Messrs. WARNER, BARNES & COMPANY,
    Legaspi:

Upon the receipt of this you will cause to be paid to Chino Vicente Go Chuangco the sum of $1,000.00, and charge it up to me.

Yours, etc.,
(Sgd.)   JUAN ACUÑA.

---

(3) LIGAO, *May 10th, 1900.*
Messrs. WARNER, BARNES & COMPANY:

Upon receipt of this you will cause to be paid to Chino Lo Quioco the sum of $2,000.00, and charge the same to me.

Yours, etc.,
(Sgd.)   JUAN ACUÑA.

---

(5) LIGAO, *May 18th, 1900.*
Messrs. WARNER, BARNES & COMPANY,
    Legaspi:

I respond to yours of the 14th of the present month, giving you receipt for the $1,000.00 that you sent me.

I have the pleasure of enclosing the receipts that you asked for, $594.41, No. 32; $83.68 No. 37; $2,733.13, No. 36.

I recommend to you my three drafts of the 10th inst. of the total
value of $3,700.00 in favor of various parties, deducting this amount,
as also those of the 2d and 8th inst., for the same object, from the proceeds of my hemp, sending me a general liquidation of my accounts for
my information and the money left. I hope you will kindly send it to
me by the bearer, whom you already know, so I can proceed in my
purchase.

Yours, etc.,

(Sgd.)   JUAN ACUÑA.

---

(6)   WARNER, BARNES & COMPANY,
LEGASPI, P. I., *May 24, 1900.*

Mr. JUAN ACUÑA, *Ligao:*

We have the pleasure to enclose liquidation notes of your account
with this company up to this date, which balance is $4,290.60. We
send in cash $1,000.00 and a receipt in your favor of $3,290.60, which
we hope will meet with your approval.

Yours, etc.,

(Signed)   WARNER, BARNES.
A. JOSÉ SILVAS.

---

(7)   WARNER, BARNES & COMPANY, ALBAY,
Legaspi, May 30, 1900.

Mr. RAMÓN SANTOS.

DEAR SIR AND FRIEND: I have in my possession yours of the 25th
inst., and I am really sorry for what has happened with your hemp. I
write to you from Ligao, where I have been since the 28th. I had a
long conference with the chief here, and he guaranteed me that nothing
would be done against you, your property and hemp, and he offers all
the considerations worthy of your person if you decide to come in the
town; and your companions, may God inspire them to set aside that
decision, avoiding the displeasure of their many friends and tears and
blood of this province, already unhappy enough.

Tell Mr. V. B. that there is no other remedy, and if you go ahead
it would be the death and ruin of the peaceful-working people that
are in the mountains, as the armed people escape every time the troops
go out, leaving those poor peaceful citizens to be sacrificed in their
stead, and especially for a lost cause that can only be saved by good
policy in showing that the Filipino people are able to govern themselves.

The colonel has come back from Manila, but he did not bring what
I told you; but a term will soon be given for all those that want to
surrender, and after that term is over everybody that remains in arms
will be declared outlaws and will be run down and killed by the
troops, to the sorrow of their friends.

I do not want to criticise your ideas as nationalist, but it would not
be just to expose all these peaceful people to a sure death and persecu-
tion; so come in, and do what you can to encourage Mr. V. B. and the
other chiefs to do the same.

A person of reputation and influence will be sent to the civil commission, which is establishing peace, to talk about the best form of government for the Philippines.

I will do all I can for your hemp at Viginillas. If the Englishman does not want it I will refer it to Ballester and Puygres. I do not know if he has much hemp on hand, but he pays $18.

(Unfinished.)

---

(8)   JUNE 20TH, 1900.

MY DEAR PACO: In answer to your welcome letter of to-day, your friend has in his possession the receipt for $3,270.60 from Warner, Barnes & Co. The bills are to be paid before the date of the last liquidation of Warner, Barnes & Co., as it is manifested in the ones your friends have in Legaspi, that is, the ones he has received from Juan Acuña, resulting in debt to Warner, Barnes & Co. $409.40, difference against him for the three bills of $3,700.00 issued with an anticipated date to attempt what I told you when I sent you the copies, and if you look over my letters in which I told you the cause of having dated said bill before the date of issue, that is, when Ligao was occupied by the Americans, Juan Acuña was an imaginary person, a supposed merchant, the one that has that name, you will readily understand is not a merchant nor a capitalist. The advanced date of the bills and accounts was made to save your interests and your friend, as you have recommended. Your private accounts and funds in Ligao in charge of your friend are $494.70. Of that sum he paid to Manay $50.00, to Mr. J. Nicolas $80.00, to Ticay $25.00, leaving $359.70. He has no money now, but if you want a letter from Legaspi he will send it to you; if not, when funds come from Legaspi, he will send it to you. The funds, $3,700.00, the value of the accounts with Warner, Barnes & Co., are in possession of your friend's representative in Legaspi. When you sent for $2,000.00 we could not send them, and your friend wrote to his representative in Legaspi to turn over to Juan Acuña the $2,000.00 that disappeared in the wagons of the Americans, as I told you before in one of my letters.

He sent Juan as a person of our entire confidence, and he did what he never did before—he accompanied the American convoy, and the $2,000.00 disappeared. The two times that he brought money from Legaspi, the Americans being already here, nothing has happened—once, on the 15th, $1,000.00, and once, on the 26th of May, $1,000.00. The representative of your friend in Legaspi advised Juan not to go with the convoy, foreseeing the danger and knowing what big thieves these people are, but he did not take his advice, and came out with them, and the misfortune happened, and more—cost him long days in prison, and also the Spaniard, Señor Azcuve, after stealing the money from him. The representative of your friend is defending the case, but he can not advance anything with the colonel of the Americans.

May God free us of these misfortunes that are weighing over the Filipino people.

Yours, etc.,

(Sgd.)   LUIS PEREZ.

(11)   WARNER, BARNES & COMPANY, ALBAY,
Legaspi, August 13, 1900.

Mr. RAMÓN SANTOS, *Ligao.*

DEAR SIR: We have received yours of the 28th of July, which received our prompt attention.

We suppose you have seen by our last letter that the sum of $409.40 is against you in our books, as Mr. López has not paid said sum. In case he is responsible for it write him so that he will pay the small amount, but for our part you know we are in no hurry for as small an amount as that, and even if it was bigger.

We have noted your order about not cashing any bills that did not bear your correct signature of Don José A. del Rosario.

Yours, etc.,

For WARNER, BARNES & Co., Limited,
(Sgd.)   ALBERT E. LAUNDERS, *Manager.*

Kb.

From record book, filed 0–4.—Licenses for steam vessels to trade in ports under control of the insurgent government. Stubs show that from December 5, 1898, to February 4, 1899, ninety-four passes were issued. These stubs are all signed by E. Aguinaldo or by his secretary of the treasury. Such licenses as may have been issued after the outbreak of hostilities with the United States were probably drawn up upon a different form; at least, they do not appear in this book. In it appears record of licenses issued to the Compañía Marítima, of Manila, January 25, 1899, in accordance with the application of its manager.

[Translation.]

(Stub.)

Number ——.

Office of the president of the revolutionary government of the Philippines:

The steamship ——, property of Señor —— ——, of —— tonnage, whose tonnage dues have been paid by the owner, is hereby authorized to make voyages and touch at the ports under control of this government, and to load and unload in them as long as said vessel does not fly the Spanish flag nor transport foreign troops, including the Spanish, and complies with the regulations of this government.

Malolos, ——, 1898.

The license itself consists of the same form as the stub, except that it closes with the words "The president," showing that it was to be signed by him.

Núm. ——

PRESIDENCIA

DEL

GOBIERNO REVOLUCIONA-
RIO DE FILIPINAS.

Por la presente queda autorizado el vapor —— de la propiedad del Señor ——
de á —— —— de carga y
cuyos derechos de tonelaje fueron pagados por su dueño, para
que pueda hacer viajes, y tocar
en los puertos de la dominación
de este Gobierno, haciendo en
los mismos las faenas de carga y
descarga, siempre que no lleve
bandera española, ni trasporte
tropas extranjeras, inclusas las
españolas, y cumpla con las disposiciones de este Gobierno.
Malolos —— de —— de 1898.

GOBIERNO REVOLUCIONARIO
Imp. bajo la dirección del Sr. Z. Fajardo.

Núm. ——

PRESIDENCIA

DEL

GOBIERNO REVOLUCIONARIO

DE

FILIPINAS.

Por la presente queda autorizado el vapor
—— de la propiedad del Señor ——
—— de á —— —— de carga y cuyos
derechos de tonelaje fueron pagados por su
dueño, para que pueda hacer viajes, y tocar
en los puertos de la dominación de este Gobierno, haciendo en los mismos las faenas
de carga y descarga, siempre que no lleve
bandera española, ni trasporte tropas extranjeras, inclusas las españolas, y cumpla
con las disposiciones de este Gobierno.
Malolos —— de —— de 189—.
El Presidente.

[Original filed, Nos. 1273–4, Philippine Insurgent Records.]

APRIL 22, 1899.

Ordinal No., 113; entry No., 369; item, remittances from the spl. loan agent of Sorsogón; detailed receipts, Sr. Amando Airán, military governor of Sorsogón, on behalf of the special loan agent of the same, Mr. Bernardino Monreal for various bonds of the loan subscribed to by various residents of that province, details as to the drafts being given below:

No. 2300 sight order of Mariano Trias on Inchausti & Co., Manila $240.00
2301 " " " " " " " " 980.00
2303 " " " " " " " " 1,200.00
2306 " " " " " " " " 846.00
2311 " " " " " " " " 200.00
2312 " " " " " " " " 400.00
50 " " " " " " Mendezona & Co., " 7,697.50
56 8 ds/s " " " " " " " 2,000.00
154 " " " " " " Smith, Bell & Co. " 1,600.00
1 3 d/s " " " " " Ambrosio Monton, " 5,400.00
9 sight " " " " " Angel Ortiz, " 600.00
12 " " " " " " " 590.00
2310 3 d/s " " Silvestre Legaspi on Inchausti & Co., " 1,000.00
10 sight " " " " " Angel Ortiz, " 1,000.00
58 8 d/s " " " " " Mendezona, " 1,000.00
In silver 246.50

$25,000.00

[Original filed, No. 256-6, Philippine Insurgent Records.]

No. 6.—I have the honor to transmit to you two drafts for the sum of $2,302.31, issued in favor of the citizen Mr. Rogaciano Rodríguez, as representing five per cent of the import and indirect export duties

6224—03——5

on the cargo of the schooner brig "Julia" of the firm of Messrs. Smith, Bell and Co. Kindly acknowledge receipt hereof.

God preserve you many years.

Tacloban, January 5, 1899.

[SEAL.]   VICENTE LUCBAN.

To the PRESIDENT OF THE PHILIPPINE REPUBLIC.

[Original filed, No. 1064–2, Philippine Insurgent Records.]

The honorable president of the revolutionary government of Malolos:

I. H. Osmond, a British subject, representative of Messrs. Smith, Bell and Co., of the trade of Manila, desires to obtain the authority mentioned in article 1 of the decree of November 30th last, in order to be able to continue to gather and export abacá and other native prodncts in this province of Albay, as well as to import and sell native and foreign goods for the account of said gentlemen, under the conditions established in that provision.

And in order to secure the same, he prays the president of the revolutionary government of Malolos, considering this petition presented within the legal period, to grant the authority mentioned, a favor which the petitioner hopes he deserves from your known kindness.

Legaspi, December 27, 1898.

I. H. OSMOND.

[P. I. R. Original filed, 1283.]

[Memorandum of La Compañía Marítima.]

MANILA, *October 15, 1898.*

To Mr. EMILIO AGUINALDO,

President of the Philippine Republic, Malolos.

MY ESTEEMED FRIEND: Although up to the present time the steamers which I manage under the American flag have not been molested by the representatives of your government in the provinces, in order to provide against their being treated as the "Dos Hermanos" was, I beg of you to send me a pass for the steamer "España" which sails to-morrow for Gubat, Tabaco, and Legaspi, returning via Sorsogón. This vessel is chartered by Messrs. Smith, Bell & Co., for the round trip. As you know I fulfill my obligations with regard to duties on freight, which I will liquidate monthly.

Hoping that you will not place any difficulties in my way on this occasion, I remain,

Yours, very truly, etc.,   JOHN T. MACLEOD.

The steamer "España," of the Compañía Marítima of Manila, is authorized to touch at Gubat, Tabaco, and Albay, provided she does not carry a Spanish flag or foreign troops, including the Spanish, and complies with the provisions of this government.

MALOLOS, *October 16, 1898.*

[P. I. R. Original filed, 258-8.]

March (*1899*) (1198-11-19).—Naval officer in charge of the port of Legaspi, stating, in answer to a communication from this office, that the charges on the 2,601 bales of abacá shipped on the steamer "España" by Mr. I. H. Osmond, of the firm of Smith, Bell & Co., amount to $2,759.66 as customs duties.

[P. I. R. Original filed, 1283.]

THE PRESIDENT OF THE REVOLUTIONARY GOVERNMENT OF THE PHILIPPINES.

HONORABLE SIR: The merchant steamer "Tiksang," under the American flag, belonging to us, we have destined to the coastwise trade, this firm having branches and commercial factors at various points of the archipelago; and being obliged to send said vessel to the ports under the jurisdiction of the government of which you are the worthy president and, in compliance with the decree issued by the president, dated November 30th last:

We request you that upon the payment of the respective tonnage dues, said vessel having a net tonnage of 887 tons, you will see fit to order the issue of a pass for the steamer "Tiksang" for the purpose desired, this being a favor which we do not doubt we will receive.

Manila, January 5, 1899.

SMITH, BELL CO.

MALOLOS, *January 5, 1899.*

NOTED.—In view of the petition presented by Messrs. Smith, Bell & Co., their request is granted.

[SEAL.]

E. AGUINALDO,
The President.

[P. I. R. Original filed, 1064-1.]

SORIANO, *October 9, 1900.*

Mr. RAMON F. SANTOS, *Samson.*

RESPECTED AND DISTINGUISHED SIR: I have received your favor of the 4th instant and have carefully noted its contents.

I can not find words with which to express my great joy on learning that the news are so favorable to our cause, and especially as the rays of the sun of our independence are already reflected in the morning sky; and therefore may God and the Holy Virgin give you, the commander of our army, many years of life, for these are the ardent wishes of your unworthy "jefe de barrio."

With regard to the last prices for the abacá which you have stored in Tabaco, as week before last the firm of Smith, Bell & Co. ordered some from me, $10 current; last week, $9/2 current, with a reduction for doubtful and second class.

I have to inform you that fearing that the enemy will do me injury if they should accidentally again enter this barrio, and as purchaser, as I am, for the said firm of Smith, Bell & Co., I was obliged to ask the representative of said gentlemen for a safe conduct, in order that the enemy should not enter my poor residence under any circumstances, so that I have here a letter signed by the said representative, who appears to be Andrew Brodrick, who is the successor of Pulcher.

With reference to the receipt of that of Malilipot, do not worry, as I personally will go and demand it and send you the said receipt there afterwards. (?)

Last Sunday, the 7th instant, I went to Ligaw for the purpose of seeing the condition of my poor house, which is certainly rather injured; and while there I saw the enemy, who appear to be rather cowardly, and according to a report of Esteban Delgado, they do not want to take any more prisoners as formerly.

It is with great regret that I have to inform you that the government of this barrio is very bad, as Señor Pio Memay, lieutenant of Sandata-han, notwithstanding the fact that he often without good cause inflicts excessive punishments upon the soldiers, I do not interfere or say anything to him, because I see that he does not even respect his captain, much less if he is drunk. There is nothing special in this for me except that I see bad results to follow, which God forbid. In addition hereto I have several times heard with my own ears said gentleman say that I had nothing to do with this barrio, either as lieutenant or cabeza, because they, and they alone, are vested with authority as military men; that is to say, they assume the civil as well as the military authority, and I believe that these words are nothing but a revenge, but without good cause. All this I set aside, but what I desire is that we should not lack people about here, as I know positively that many are about to leave this barrio only in order to avoid being unjustly maltreated, and I therefore inform you of the facts in order that you may take the proper action.

I have furnished Mr. Calleja a form of the statement upon which to enter the names of the persons of whom export duties have been collected, as you instruct me in your said favor.

Without anything further for the present and with regards to you and our old man and all the gentlemen and friends there, dispose unconditionally of your devoted and unworthy servant, who, with the greatest consideration, subscribes your affectionate and attentive servant, who kisses your hands.

VICTORIANO DEL CASTILLO.

NOTE.—Santos was a colonel in the insurgent force in Albay Province. "Our old man" refers, undoubtedly, to the insurgent commander of the province, being a form I have seen used for that purpose.—T.

L.

[P. I. R. Original in Books B.]

HONORABLE SIR: The necessity for systematizing the administrative business of the public treasury as soon as possible imperatively calls for the drawing up of a budget, of the formation of estimates, which will be uniform, and to which the receipts and expenses, approved by the treasury, will be adjusted.

Convinced of the undoubted need of this, the secretary who signs this document has drawn up the accompanying schedule of general and local estimates for the present year of 1899, and has the honor to present them to you, in order that by the proper course they may become law.

He does not disguise the fact that more than once during their compilation doubt and distrust, the result of a profound conviction of his own inadequacy, to say nothing of the entire absence of the data so necessary for a work of this kind, an absence which although explicable when the incipient organization of the public service is taken into consideration, has made him hesitate before an undertaking neither simple nor possible in the brief period of our government's existence.

Putting aside these considerations, the main idea taken into account has been the abnormal present condition of the country, due to the late war and that now taking place in Manila. The present condition of the country undoubtedly affects the government's expenditures and receipts, and this is shown by the increase or diminution of one or the other, favorably or otherwise. Unfortunately those which we must consider in this estimate are of the latter nature, hence, taking under consideration the question of expenses, those of the department of war are greater than they would normally be in time of peace; and more than one-half of the total receipts have been assigned for this purpose. On account of what may happen in this new war against the North American nation we have to maintain a large portion of the army on a war footing, and this necessity requires a great part of our resources, withdrawing large sums which would otherwise permit us to meet other obligations of the government. Were this not allowed, our most valued and holy honor and national integrity, which can only be saved by force of arms, would be endangered.

In view of this consideration, the salaries of the military and civil officials are reduced in the estimate. They are cut down to simple allowances, and are taken as a model for those of civil officials. thus equalizing the remuneration of the corresponding classes of those who serve the government. It is proper to mention with regard to civil officials that the schedule of personal service in the bill must be considered as temporary until all branches of the active administration are definitely organized by means of the laws which are being decreed.

As a result, then, of the abnormal condition of the country, we find a considerable reduction in receipts for the present year, which are calculated at $6,342,407, and which, compared with those of the budget of the late Spanish Government, corresponding to the fiscal year of 1896–97, which amounted to $17,474,020, show an approximate falling off of 36 per cent. This is not strange, nor should this falling off appear over-estimated when to the abnormal condition of the country another and no less important condition is added, that is that in the bill the tax of vassalage upon non-Christian and savage tribes, the import duties in Luzon and adjacent islands, and the numerous sources of income represented by granting licenses for gambling, are all abolished, and lastly, the occupation of Manila by the Army of the United States. As for the tax of vassalage upon non-Christian and savage tribes, its abolition is perfectly justified, as it is ill adapted to the new Philippine régime, inspired as it is by the holy ideals of equality and fraternity, and placed under the august shadow of the newly established republic.

This odious tax would no doubt have some reason for existence under the Spanish Government, but now it can not exist, because it is in violation of our institutions and would be in direct opposition to the frank policy of attraction which we have declared, and which fortunately is already giving very satisfactory results. As a proof, witness the spontaneous adhesion to our Government of thousands of men who but a short time ago were in opposition to the civil authority, and, owing to the disastrous policy pursued under the late Spanish rule and the refusal of the clerical dominators to adopt methods of conciliation, were being driven farther and farther from the pale of the community.

Reasons of state and justice demand, then, the abolition of vassalage, and by its repeal the present taxes, which now weigh heavily on the rest of the people, will later be extended to those new citizens, when they participate equally in the benefits enjoyed by the others.

The present suspension of import duties in Luzon and the adjacent islands is dictated by the fact that the custom-house at Manila is not now in the possession of our government, and although those duties could be demanded in other ports of Luzon, which might be so used, their exaction is neither convenient nor politic at present, the object being to give free entry to foreign products, and above all to articles of prime necessity, and in this way to alleviate as soon as possible the economical crisis which the late war has left as a melancholy legacy to the country, and also to prevent the possibility of another.

As regards the suppression of the receipts from licenses for gambling and taxes on cockfights, it may be considered perfectly justified. As long as all gambling is to be considered criminal under rule 3 of the decree of June 20 last year concerning the government of provinces and towns, no returns can be counted on from these sources.

Another of the contributing causes of the diminution of the receipts is the military occupation of Manila. Manila, the emporium of the wealth, the center of the commerce, the most important port, with the largest population in the archipelago, is the principal source of revenue to the Philippine treasury. This source has been exploited and depleted by a foreign government, and so plainly do our receipts show the effect of this, that without any doubt 33 per cent of the reduction of our resources is the direct result of that exploitation.

I shall now proceed to consider the probable receipts of the treasury. The fear of going to extremes in the matter of taxation, and, moreover, in obedience to the concluding precepts of the constitution and the instructions for the government of provinces and towns, which, in article 94, temporary provisions, and article 32, respectively, ordain that the laws in use before the emancipation shall continue in force in these islands, and also that chiefs of the towns should take charge of all local taxes imposed by the Spanish Government, have moved the undersigned to accept, at least for the present, all the sources of income of the said government, with the exception of those taxes whose abolition was caused by the actual circumstances, for the reasons already given.

In order to find some equivalent for the losses caused by this repeal, the taxes on transport and export ordained by decree of October 7, and modified by another decree of November 16, last year, are retained.

A war tax, justified by the present need, is likewise imposed in place of the personal cédula, which, on account of the general antipathy felt toward it, is deemed wise to abolish. This is divided into classes. The amount to be paid by each is given in the bill.

As a new source of income, however, the property of the religious corporations enters into the bill by virtue of the sole additional article of the constitution, and are considered restored to the State; this, however, will not be a bar to future adjudications concerning the claims of private individuals. An intelligent and honest administration of these estates, or, in default of this, their lease, will undoubtedly yield (to the treasury) an income of no slight importance.

With regard to sources of income of a local character, excepting the proceeds from games and cockfights, those in use by the late Spanish Government are retained, and, in addition, a tax of 50 per cent on the cost of solemn burial services, permits for festivals, and 1 céntimo on each pound of meat is imposed. These taxes can be paid without any great sacrifice in the towns where they are in force.

And, as authorized by rules 35, 36, and the last paragraph of rule 44 of the orders I have referred to so many times, juntas and provincial committees may collect fees on each civil case, the importance of which is determined by the first of said rules; publishing bans of marriage; for marriages; for entry in the civil registry, and on landed estates owned in the towns, thus adding receipts from these different sources to the bill.

Lastly, for the necessary separation of expenditures, from general and local receipts, the former are specified in sections A and B, the latter in sections C and D, details of which are indicated in the respective sections of each article.

Before concluding the secretary, who signs, desires to state that although the functions and duties of the various organisms of the central, provincial, and local administration of the treasury can not be so well defined as by a separate law, he has nevertheless thought fit to sacrifice the usual order for the sake of a more prompt and speedy execution of the estimates, and to embody in the bill the more precise instructions which conduce to that end, adapting for the same the acts of the law of accountability of September 12, 1870, and the order of October 4, 1870, which are considered as in force with the existing organization authorized by the order of June 20 last upon the government of provinces and towns.

Founded, as it is, upon the principles before mentioned, the undersigned has the honor to submit to you herewith the draft of the proposed law.

Malolos, February 12, 1899.

THE SECRETARY OF TREASURY,
Per ARCADIO ROSARIO.

* * * *

LAW.

Emilio Aguinaldo y Famy, president of the Philippine Republic.

Know all men that the congress of representatives has provisionally voted and approved, and that I have sanctioned and ordered the promulgation of the following:

ARTICLE 1. The expenses of the government for the present year of 1899 are fixed at $6,324,729.38, distributed by sections, chapters, and articles, as per itemized account given in Exhibit A attached.

ART. 2. It is estimated that the receipts to meet the obligations of the government for the year mentioned will be $6,342,407 as per Exhibit B.

ART. 3. The expenditures from local funds for the year are fixed at $704,602, as set forth in Exhibit C.

ART. 4. Local receipts for the same period are computed at $826,900.

ART. 5. While the war lasts all taxes and sources of income established by the Spanish Government will be continued, the collection and administration of which shall be subject to the same rules, directions, and regulations as have been issued for that purpose; but this will not be construed as preventing such reforms as the government may establish, in accordance with the provisions of article 94 of the constitution, and provided they do not conflict with the laws and decrees in force.

ART. 6. The tax of vassalage on savage and non-Christian tribes is hereby abolished, as well as the discount on the salaries of all employés.

ART. 7. The collection of personal cédulas is meanwhile suspended, and in its place a special war tax is imposed, of a temporary nature, which will be based upon property holdings and called a "Certificate of citizenship." Amounts which have been already collected at the time of imposing the new tax shall be deducted.

ART. 8. This tax is divided into the following classes:

Class 1	$100.00	Class 5	$5.00
Class 2	50.00	Class 6	2.00
Class 3	25.00	Class 7	1.00
Class 4	10.00	Class 8	Free.

Class 1 includes all persons owning, controlling, or managing a capital in money or property to the value of over $25,000.

Class 2, those owning, etc., property or money, $15,001 to $25,000.

Class 3, those owning, etc., property or money, $10,001 to $15,000.

Class 4, those owning, etc., property or money, $5,001 to $10,000.

Class 5, those owning, etc., property or money, $1,001 to $5,000.

Class 6 includes all males over 18 not included in the above classes.

Class 7, all women over 18.

Class 8, free, includes soldiers and military employés in active service; those over 60; the poor, and those physically and mentally incapable of performing labor.

Said taxes will be collected in two semi-annual installments in advance by the cabezas of the respective barrios, and in accordance with the poll list.

ART. 9. During this year import duties in Luzon and the adjacent islands are to be abolished; duties on exportation and coastwise trade will remain as heretofore, on a ten per cent ad valorem schedule.

ART. 10. The duties on exportation and coastwise trade referred to in article 9 will be collected by the "consejeros de rentas"[a] (provincial treasurers or tax commissioners), acting as collectors of customs, in those ports which are the capitals of the provinces. In other places the collection of the duties will be in charge of "delegados de rentas"[b] (local treasurers or tax collectors), under the immediate supervision of the local "juntas" (boards composed of the four principal officers of a town and the "cabezas" of each "barrio"), the presidente of which must remit weekly to the provincial treasury the amount collected during the week.

ART. 11. The property of religious corporations restored to the

---

[a] Members of provincial council charged with the collection of taxes, etc.
[b] Members of local boards charged with the collection of taxes, etc.

state in accordance with the additional article of the constitution will be administered by men of means who will be designated by the secretary of the treasury, local chiefs (presidentes) preferred, who will furnish such security, in cash or by bond, as the secretary of the treasury may deem necessary.

Art. 12. Those who administer the property of religious corporations will receive in payment for their services a percentage of the annual rent received from the property; same to be payable when they have rendered accounts with the corresponding vouchers of all receipts and expenditures during the year, in addition to the quarterly account they must render to the secretary of the treasury. Fees for administration granted by this article shall be as follows:

$1 to $100: Fee of 20 per cent.

$101 to $1,000: Fee of 20 per cent for first 100 pesos, plus 15 per cent for remainder.

$1,001 to $10,000 and over: 20 per cent for first 100 pesos, plus 15 per cent for remainder, up to 1,000 pesos; plus 10 per cent for remainder.

Art. 13. In default of responsible persons who can deposit the requisite security the government and the local "junta" will simultaneously receive bids for the lease of the said estates, in accordance with the general instructions of the government and the special one that the lease price shall be at least half of the annual rental which was paid for the land before it was restored to the state, and also that the price of the subleases, if any be made, shall not exceed two-thirds of the amount which the lessees paid to the former owners, preference being given to the present occupants.

Art. 14. For the use of the municipal treasury there is hereby created a tax of 50 per cent on permits for solemn burial ceremonies, as well as a tax of 2 pesos for each license for a festival and one of 1 centimo for each pound of meat, which taxes will be collected by the "delegado de rentas" (member of the city council charged with the collection of revenue), and in his default by the "contratistas" (contractor for the purpose of supplying meat to a town; only one was allowed).

Art. 15. All civil or military employés of whatever rank, from the highest to the lowest, shall henceforth receive the pay indicated in the following table:

Military.	Civil.	
Lieutenant-general	Secretaries	720
General of division	Chief of bureau	600
General of brigade	Asst. chief of bureau, 1st class	540
Colonel	Asst. chief of bureau, 2d class	480
Lieutenant-colonel	Asst. chief of division	420
Major	Clerk, first class	360
Captain	Clerk, second class	300
First lieutenant	Clerk, third class	240
Second lieutenant	Clerk, fourth class	180
Sergeant	Employés receiving 2½ chupas of rice (a little over 1⅜ pints).	72
Corporal, at $4.50 per month	Employés receiving 2½ chupas of rice	54
Soldiers, at $3.60 per month	....do	42

Art. 16. No payment will be authorized which is not included in the present estimates or granted by later authority, given in conformity with the law of accountability (ley de contabilidad) of Septem-

ber 12, 1870, and order of October 4, of the same year, which are continued in force temporarily, in so far as they are not contrary to laws of the republic.

ART. 17. Provincial councils shall be provided with a secure safe with three keys or padlocks, one of which will be in the custody of the head of the province (jefe provincial), one in the custody of the member of the council charged with the collection of revenue (consejero de rentas), and one in the custody of the member charged with legal affairs (consejero de justicia).

ART. 18. No official shall be allowed to receive two salaries, even though he holds more than one office.

ART. 19. The secretary of the treasury will have authority and control over all offices and affairs of his department, and his duties are:

A. To secure the most equitable distribution of contributions and imposts, the amounts received from taxation, and suggest to the government suitable alterations and ameliorations.

B. To approve the general accounts of receipts and disbursements which the chief of the division of taxes and the chief disbursing officer (ordenador-general) may render, and see that the monthly reports of receipts and expenditures by the officials of the several bureaus are forwarded to him.

C. To prepare the estimate of receipts and expenses.

D. To provide for deficiencies or extraordinary credits, with the consent of the cabinet, if the urgency of the case will not permit the passage of a special law.

ART. 20. It is the duty of the chief disbursing officer (ordenador-general de pagos):

A. To make payments and to liquidate all obligations and liabilities of the government, either himself or through deputies, except in those of the war and navy departments.

B. To arrange monthly for the distribution of funds in accordance with the sections of the general estimate (budget) of the government, opening the necessary credits for the provincial treasuries for the expenses of the following month, and

C. To see that the provincial presidentes render their accounts of public expenses with punctuality, which, after they have audited, corrected, and consolidated in a general return, he will forward to the secretary of the treasury.

ART. 21. The chief of the division of direct and indirect taxation shall have charge of the preparation, coursing, and closing up of all operations leading up to the examination, declaration, and liquidation of all treasury dues, subject to the instructions, rules, and regulations, and therefore his duties are:

A. To see that the taxes, imposts, and other revenues of the government are collected on the day and at the time designated, and that their payment into the treasury is not delayed..

B. To administer and sell, *in conformity with the laws*, property of the state, as well as, in accordance with (orders of) the cabinet, the property seized on account of offenses or for any other reason.

C. To keep in security the stamped paper of the government, the custodian of which will render him an account of that department.

D. To see that the members of provincial councils charged with the collection of revenues (consejeros de rentas) render accounts of public revenue and stamped paper with punctuality; these he will examine, correct, and consolidate into one general amount, which he will forward to the secretary of the treasury.

E. To obey, and to see that all employees under his jurisdiction obey, the laws, regulations, and instructions, and orders now in force, as well as those which may hereafter be enacted.

ART. 22. The duties of the auditor-general (interventor-general) for the government are:

A. To scrutinize all acts of the administration in regard to the schedule of taxes and rates of duty and the collection and apportionment of the income of the state.

B. To supervise the accounting for payments and receipts.

C. To have charge of the general bookkeeping system of all departments.

D. To submit to the secretary of the treasury the annual accounts and the general returns of receipts and expenditures.

E. He will himself, personally, or by means of deputies, inspect all the bureaus and divisions in the department of war and navy in so far as refers to matters which require settlement and payment.

ART. 23. The functions and duties of the treasurer (tesorero de la secretaria de hacienda) are:

A. To safeguard the public funds.

B. To collect the amount derived from taxes and other sources of revenue, and to sign the vouchers issued as receipts of payment to persons concerned.

C. To pay treasury bills or warrants issued by the chief disbursing officer (ordenador) and countersigned by his assistant. No payment will be made which is not included in the estimates unless injury to the state and especially to the liberty of the country would result from delay, in which case it will suffice if the civil and military authority of the place where the necessity has arisen should issue an order on the treasurer and auditor-general, so that the payment can be made under responsibility of said authority.

D. To see that officials in charge of provincial or subtreasuries render accounts, which he will examine, correct, and consolidate into a general account, which he will submit to the secretary of the treasury, together with the several accounts which compose it.

E. To carry an account and record of all receipts and disbursements of public funds.

ART. 24. Members of the provincial councils who are charged with the collection of revenue (consejeros de rentas) will for the present discharge the same duties as former treasury officials under Spanish government, and consequently their duties are:

A. To collect taxes and contributions and to make payments on the warrants and orders of the local head.

B. To render accounts of money, taxes, and stamped paper and forward them to the secretary of the treasury.

C. To keep and audit the accounts of all receipts and disbursements of their several offices.

ART. 25. The heads of provinces will, for the present, be the deputies of the chief disbursing officer (ordenador general de pagos) and as such will have the following duties:

A. To draw up in advance the estimates of expenses for the next succeeding month and make a request on the secretary of the treasury for the amount necessary, in order that the latter may make proper allowance for same in the apportionment of funds.

Art. 26. The members of provincial councils charged with legal affairs (consejeros de justicia), who, for the present, will discharge the duties of auditors of the treasury, will perform the same functions and service as prescribed for auditors-general in article 22, with the exception of the duties described in paragraphs D and E.

Art. 27. The local treasurers (delegados de rentas)—members of town council charged with collection of taxes, etc.—as the auxiliary agents of the acting provincial treasurers, should—

A. Attend to the collection of taxes and imposts in their district, and after deducting payments ordered by the member of the provincial council charged with the collection of revenues, will remit the balance of the funds to the provincial treasury, and

B. Keep an account and record of disbursement of funds with an explanation of each entry.

Art. 28. It shall be the duty of the member of the provincial council charged with the collecting of revenues (acting provincial treasurer) to render treasury accounts, giving a statement of receipts and disbursements, as well as accounts of public funds. And it shall likewise be the duty of the provincial presidente (governor) to render an account of public expenses, each of which, after being checked by the member of the provincial council charged with legal affairs (consejero de justicia—acting provincial auditor), will be sent in duplicate to the secretary of the treasury for examination and final audit.

Art. 29. In case of the absence or legal incapacity of the head of the province the vice-president, who is the local chief of the capital of the province (Cabecera), will act in his place. In case of the absence of the member of the provincial council charged with the collection of taxes (consejero de rentas) the corresponding officer in the local board of the capital of the province will act in his place. In case of the absence of the member of the provincial council charged with legal matters (consejero de justicia) the corresponding member of the local board of the provincial capital will perform his duties. The substitutes will receive half of the allowances assigned in the estimates to the permanent occupants of the positions, provided the vacancy is only temporary, and will receive the full allowance when the absence is permanent, unless it is on the public service.

All employés whose state of health is such as to prevent them from performing their work, may make formal application for a leave of absence, enclosing certificates showing their ill health. These will be forwarded to the chief of the branch to which they belong, who will pass upon their request.

Sick leaves may be granted for one month and extended to two, if the employé can prove that his illness continues. If he has not returned to duty at the expiration of such period, the employé will lose his position and all right to salary or allowances. Leave shall be considered as beginning on the day following that on which the employé receives notice of it having been granted. Heads of provinces can grant sick leaves on notifying the head of the department to which the application belongs for his information. They may also grant leaves of absence for one month to employés on private business, with an extension of fifteen days, but during this period said employés will not receive pay or allowances.

ART. 31. The officials, who together hold the keys of the cash boxes, that are described in article 17, will, on the first day of each month, proceed to count the sum or sums in their charge, making an itemized statement in triplicate, two copies of which they will forward to the secretary of the treasury.

These officials will take charge of all stamped paper which the corresponding bureau of the treasury forwards, and will keep a special book for the purpose of accounting for it. In order to issue this stamped paper they are authorized to appoint salesmen who will receive the same and pay for it in advance, less their own allowance for selling same.

ART. 32. The three officials above described are also authorized to receive and enter in the treasury all voluntary deposits of individuals who desire to guarantee some business transaction (probably means security for performance of contracts, which security under Spanish law was deposited in cash).

ART. 33. If from unforeseen causes the receipts are not sufficient to meet the expenses reckoned upon in the estimates, by the order which gives precedence to the needs of the public service, all salaries shall be stopped, and employés will be allowed only sufficient for the necessities of life, which will be met as far as the resources of the public treasury admit.

Malolos, February 19, 1899.

EMILIO AGUINALDO.

The Secretary of the Treasury, per

ARCADIO ROSARIO.

(NOTE.—The estimates in detail follow in the original.)

M.

CONTRIBUTIONS OF WAR.

Ilogan, December 15, 1898 (289–3).—Special tax commissioner reports that he expects the contribution of war of Isabela province to be $100,000 in 1899, to be paid in two installments, in September and July, 1899.

Bautista, February 9, 1899 (49–1).—C. M. Clark, agent for Smith, Bell & Co., sends T. Sandico a carload of rice, which he desires him to present to President Aguinaldo for his force.

Malolos, February 10, 1899 (289–1).—Baldomero Aguinaldo, secretary of war, in a circular letter informs the people that when the present conditions (war with the Americans) cease contributions given for the war or their value will be returned.

Gerona, Tarlac, February 10, 1899 (289–11).—Report from collector of contributions of war that he has received 95 sacks of rice as a donation from Smith, Bell & Co. (Bautista).

Malolos, February 11, 1899 (49–1).—The commissary of war receipts for the above rice.

Bayambang, Pangasinan Province, February 18, 1899 (289–11).—
Report from collector of contributions that Smith, Bell & Co. have
given 100 sacks of rice as a voluntary contribution of war.

Bautista, February 18, 1899 (258–4).—C. M. Clark, agent for Smith,
Bell & Co., to F. Macabulos, asking authority to bring palay from
Camiling.

Bautista, March 7, 1899 (258–3).—C. M. Clark, agent for Smith,
Bell & Co., sends General Macabulos 111 sacks of rice.

Isabela de Luzon, March 14, 1899 (297–3).—Forwards $36,816.77,
contributions of war.

Bayambang, Pangasinan, March 15, 1899 (289–11).—Agent for
Smith, Bell & Co. contributes 100 sacks of rice to revolutionary
government.

Malolos, October 7, 1899 (247–1).—Roll of commissioners appointed
to collect contributions of war; 25 commissioners consigned to Manila,
Bulacan, Laguna, Batangas, Bataan, Nueva Ecija, Pampanga, Mòrong,
Ambos Ilocos, Pangasinan, Cagayan, Isabela, Zambales, Albay, Capiz,
and Antique provinces, the last two in Panay and the others in Luzòn
Island.

Nueva Cáceres, October 18, 1899 (721–6).—Telegram from delegate
at Camarines and Albay (loan to secretary of treasury) states that in
January and February he sent $100,000 to secretary of treasury from
Smith, Bell & Co., by conduct of Maj. Sanreano Cruz, of Albay.

Atimonan, October 28, 1899 (526–8).—Gen. J. I. Paua informs
Aguinaldo that he is forwarding 220,000 pesos from Tayabas Province, through the general commanding the political-military government of southern Luzon. Paua states that since May 18 last he has
forwarded about 400,000 pesos to the treasury.

[Original filed 1273–8.]

[Translation.]

Office of the Secretary of the Treasury.—General estimate of expenses for 1899.—
No. 464.

(Voucher—Warrant.)

Mr. MAURICIO ILAGAN,
Paymaster-General of the Filipino Republic.

Documents which accompany.	The treasurer-general is hereby directed to pay to Mr. Ramon Soriano, lieutenant-colonel of infantry,

Documents which accompany.

The certification referred to.

Paid
Total—$178,642.33

The treasurer-general is hereby directed to pay to
Mr. Ramon Soriano, lieutenant-colonel of infantry,
the sum of one hundred seventy-eight thousand, six
hundred forty-two pesos and thirty-three céntimos
in drafts and letters of exchange, in order to negotiate the exchange of the same for cash in Manila, by
order of the honorable Mr. President, the bearers of,
the same being Francisco Enaje and Lorenzo Sanchez, whose certification accompanies.

And in virtue of this warrant, with the receipt of the party named,
and the corresponding entries of the transaction by the paymaster's
clerk and the comptroller, the stipulated amount will be payable to him
in the corresponding office of the treasury.

Tarlac, 5th of August, 1899. P. S.
Entered. Bookkeeper of the paymaster-general.

Entered. Chief of bookkeeping department.

Paid. Received. R. Soriano.

Mr. Sinforoso San Pedro, chief of the cashier's division and central treasurer of the Filipino republic by regular substitution, certifies: l That to-day there has been paid under warrant No. 464 to Mr. Ramon Soriano, lieutenant-colonel of infantry, the sum of one hundred seventy-eight thousand six hundred forty-two pesos and thirty-three céntimos in letters of exchange and orders to be exchanged for cash in Manila, which are as follows:

No. 12.—For $590—Sorsogón, 10th of March, 1899. At sight, please pay this original draft to the order of Mr. Mariano Trias, the sum of five hundred ninety pesos, for value received, and enter the same in account as per letter of advice of your servant. For F. Suarez. Marcial Suarez. To Angel Ortiz, Manila.

No. 9.—For $600—Sorsogón, 21st of February, 1899. At sight, please pay this original draft to the order of Mr. Mariano Trias, the sum of six hundred pesos, value received, and enter the same in account as per letter of advice. By authority of F. Suarez. Marcial Suarez. To Mr. Angel Ortiz, Manila.

No. 181.—For 2,500 pesos—Calbayog, 20th of February, 1899. At three days' sight, please pay this original draft to the order of bearer the sum of two thousand five hundred pesos, which you will enter in account current according to letter of advice of Warner, Barnes & Co. R. E. Seall. To Messrs. Warner, Barnes & Co., Manila.

No. 135.—Barugo, 23rd of January, 1899—For $6,015.15. At three days' sight, please pay to the order of Mr. Teodoro Legaspi, this first letter of exchange, the sum of six thousand fifteen dollars, fifteen céntimos, for value received, which you will enter in account current of your obedient servant, A. L. Bindloss. Messrs. Warner, Barnes & Co., Manila.

137.—Barugo, 23rd of January—For $4,766.67. At three days' sight you will please pay this first of exchange to the order of Mr. Teodoro Legaspi the sum of four thousand seven hundred seventy-six dollars and sixty-seven céntimos for value received, and place the same in account current of your obedient servant, A. L. Bindloss. Messrs. Warner, Barnes & Co., Manila.

Katbalogan, 27th of March, 1899.—Messrs. Aldecoa & Co., Manila. Dear Sirs: By virture of this draft, and without further advice, you will please pay in current money to the citizen, Mr. Teodoro Legaspi, for my account, the sum of $80,761.85, eighty thousand seven hundred sixty-one pesos and eighty-five céntimos, value received here, which sum you will please pass to my debit. With thanks in anticipation, I repeat myself, your obedient servant, who kisses your hand, Fernando Escaño.

Fernando Escaño y Villareal—Leyte, Malitbog—Malitbog, 11th of February, 1899.—Messrs. Aldecoa & Co., Manila. Dear Sirs: By virtue of this letter, and without further advices, you will please pay in current money to the citizen, Mr. Teodoro Legaspi, and for my account, the sum of thirty-three thousand five hundred nine pesos and fifty-eight céntimos, which sum you will likewise please place to the debit of my account. With thanks in advance, I repeat myself, your obedient servant who kisses your hand, Fernando Escaño.

Fernando Escaño y Villareal—Leyte, Malitbog—Malitbog, 11th of February, 1899—Messrs. Aldecoa & Co., Manila. Dear Sirs: By virtue of this letter, and without further advice, you will please pay in current money to the citizen, Mr. Teodoro Legaspi, and for my account, the sum of forty-nine thousand eight hundred ninety-nine pesos and eight céntimos, which sum you will likewise pass to the debit of my account. With thanks in advance, I repeat myself, your obedient servant who kisses your hand, Fernando Escaño.

And in order that the preceding may be made evident and have the desired and necessary value and effect, this document is viséed by the secretary of the treasury, and sealed by the chief of this office in Tarlac, the 5th day of August, one thousand eight hundred and ninety-nine.

SINFOROSO SAN PEDRO.

O. K.
Secretary of the treasury.

HUGO YLAGAN.

[Seal of treasury of Philippine republic.]

NOTE.—To the drafts referred to is united a letter corresponding to drafts Nos. 9 and 12, for six hundred pesos and five hundred ninety pesos, respectively, which is as follows:

There is a note at the margin which says: Francisco Suarez—Sorsogón, 10th of March, 1899—Mr. Angel Ortiz, Manila. Dear Sir: I hereby request that you please accept and pay the following drafts: No. 9, at sight, to Mr. Mariano Trias, for the sum of 600 pesos, and No. 12, at sight, to Mr. Mariano Trias, for the sum of 590 pesos; total, 1,190 pesos, which you will please charge to the account of your obedient servant who kisses your hand. For F. Suarez. M. Suarez.

NOTE.—It is hereby certified that said documents were delivered to Mr. Ramon Soriano by order of the honorable president, he being the one charged with writing to Manila to collect the money on same, the bearers of which being Messrs. Francisco Enaje and Lorenzo Sanchez.

Tarlac, 5th of August, 1899.

SINFOROSO SAN PEDRO.

Concurs.

The secretary of treasury.

HUGO YLAGAN.
FRANCISCO ENAJE.
LORENZO SANCHEZ.

[Seal of treasury of Philippine republic.]

TRANSLATION OF PAPERS CAPTURED AT DAGUPAN.

[P. I. R. Originals filed 49–1.]

No. 1.

There is a letter head which says: "Smith, Bell & Co., Manila, Cebú, Iloilo. Telegraphic address: Bell, Manila."

BAUTISTA, February 9, 1899.

MY VERY DEAR FRIEND, SEÑOR SANDICO: I take pleasure in enclosing a shipping receipt for a carload of rice, which I hope the president, General Aguinaldo, will accept for his troops. My intention was to send white rice, but through a mistake at my storehouses they loaded uncleaned rice.

Command in everything your sincere friend, who kisses your hand.

(Signed) C. M. CLARK.

No. 2.

(Draft of a letter written on same sheet as preceding.)

To the Intendente Militar:

Enclosed herewith I have the pleasure of sending you a receipt made by the agent of the station at Gerona, hoping that you will be so kind as to arrange to have someone receive at the station in this town the hundred sacks of rice which are described on the receipt, or ticket, for the subsistence of our troops.

God, etc.

No. 3.

(Draft of a letter written on same sheet as preceding.)

MALOLOS, *February 11, 1899.*

My DEAR FRIEND: With your kind letter of the 9th instant I received the 100 sacks of rice which you voluntarily furnished for the use of the Filipino army, for which General Aguinaldo is extremely grateful, and in the name of the government I give you a million thanks. With nothing else to say, I repeat, that I am your very affectionate friend, who kisses your hand.

No. 4.

There is a letter head which says: "Intendencia militar del gobierno republicano de Filipinas."

I have received the invoice of 100 sacks of rice sent from the town of Gerona (Tarlac), furnished for the supply of the troops of our army. Of this I have the honor to inform you, in reply to your kind communication dated to-day.

May God keep you many years. Malolos, February 10, 1899.

The commissary of war.

(Signed)   PEDRO ARIGO.

To the SECRETARY OF THE INTERIOR.

No. 5.

To the SECRETARY OF THE INTERIOR:

Out of the one hundred sacks of rice referred to in your kind letter of the 10th instant, I must inform you that only ninety-five have been received in this department. They come from Bautista, having been donated by the Smith-Bell Company.

Malolos, February 11, 1899.

The officer in charge.

(Signed)   RAMON FERMÍN.

TRANSLATION OF A SERIES OF LETTERS AND DOCUMENTS CAPTURED AT DAGUPAN.

[P. I. R. Original filed 49-2.]

No. 1.

To the honorable President of the Revolutionary Government of the Philippines.

HONORABLE SIR: We have the honor to transmit to your hands two petitions from our representative in Legaspi appealing from the judgment rendered by the delegado de marina of that port, who has made him pay a tax of 5 per cent export duty on 2,446 bundles of hemp bought before the arrival of the troops of the revolutionary government. We enclose two receipts relating to said hemp.

We can not do less than protest with due respect against this tax and this procedure, and we request that you be so kind as to revoke that judgment and order that the sum paid by our representative at Legaspi be returned, taking into consideration that he bought the hemp for shipment to Manila before the new impost had been decreed, a reason which has always been valid in public administration by reason of being founded upon the principle that laws have no retroactive effect so as to take effect in the cases of acts and propositions of earlier date than that of their promulgation.

Moreover, the direct tax has always been unfavorable to agriculture and to movements and shipments from province to province because the additional tax absorbs the profits and the sources of the revenue continue to decrease instead of increase.

The provisions of international law through the administrative proceedings and the forms that should precede a new impost give grounds for a claim for damages, which we desire to avoid rather than institute.

Wherefore we request you to please render a just decision upon the petitions which we submit herewith, with the belief that we have no doubt of securing justice.

Manila, January 3, 1899.

SMITH, BELL & Co.

There are several revolutionary postage stamps, canceled with a stamp which says: "Gobno. Revolro. de Filipinas. Secreta. de Hacienda."

No. 2.

(A receipt on an official blank.)

Department of marine and commerce of the revolutionary government of the Philippines. No. 24. Province of Albay. Port of Legaspi.

Received of Mr. J. H. Osmond, the sum of one thousand three hundred and eighty-one pesos, in payment of the duty of 5 per cent on the value of his merchandise loaded upon the American steamer *Cebú*, which is bound for Manila.

Legaspi, December 26, 1898.

The administrator,

LAUREANO CRUZ.

The inspector,

LORENZO PASCUAL.

Amount, $1,381.

This sum will be turned in as a deposit.

No. 3.

Department of marine and commerce of the revolutionary government of the Philippines. No. 15. Province of Albay. Port of Legaspi.

Received of Mr. J. H. Osmond the sum of one thousand and eighty-five pesos in payment of the duty of 5 per cent on the value of his merchandise loaded upon the American steamer *Cebú*, which is bound for Manila.

Legaspi, December 9, 1898.

The administrator,   LAUREANO CRUZ.
The inspector,   LORENZO PASCUAL.

Amount, $1,085.

NOTE.—This sum will be turned into the chests of the treasury as a deposit.

SIR: Mr. J. H. Osmond, a British subject and representative of Messrs. Smith, Bell & Company, a business firm of Manila, has recourse to the authority of the general in appeal from the judgment delivered by the delegado de marina of this port of Legaspi, declaring subject to the payment of export duties 1,085 bundles of hemp, shipped to the capital, Manila, by the steamer *Cebú* consigned by me.

Nothing is further from my mind than to evade the payment of any impost that your government may establish; or still less to invoke any law or legal doctrines that may tend to nullify it. Only settle for me the point as to whether the decree that provides for the imposition of this duty should have a retroactive character or force, so as to be applicable to an article of commerce purchased before its promulgation.

I must make it clear that the 1,085 bundles shipped to Manila on the ship mentioned are a part of the 2,500 bundles bought in this port of Legaspi for the gentlemen whose names appear in the accompanying statement or note, which is a literal copy of the one presented by me voluntarily on October 17th last, to the delegado then in office, Señor Fulgencio Contreras.

Having then paid into the treasury of the government the sum of $1,085, to which the 5 per cent export duty amounted, in consequence of the demand of the present delegado, Señor Cruz,

I beg of the general to please declare exempt from said payment of duty the 2,500 bundles acquired before the establishment of this new impost; or otherwise to make a proper decision to settle said question, which is not clear to me. It is justice which I beg.

Legaspi, December 12, 1898.

J. H. OSMOND.

No. 5.

Statement of the bundles of hemp purchased from Messrs. Smith, Bell & Company before the arrival of the troops of the revolutionary government.

Bought from—	Bundles.	
Balburo Jaucian	1,500	Balance due on former contracts.
Luis Thomas	100	
Same	500	Bought on the 10th of this month.
E. Ruiz	400	
	2,500	

Daraga, October 17, 1898.

J. H. OSMOND.

No. 6.

Mr. J. H. Osmond, a British subject, and representative of Messrs. Smith, Bell & Company, a business firm of Manila, has recourse to the authority of the general in appeal from the judgment delivered by the delegado de marina of this port of Legaspi, declaring subject to the payment of export duties 1,381 bundles of hemp, shipped to the capital, Manila, by the steamer *Cebú* consigned by me.

Nothing is further from my mind than to evade the payment of any impost that your government may establish or still less to invoke any law of legal doctrine that may tend to nullify it.   Only settle for me the point as to whether the decree that provides for the imposition of this duty should have retroactive character or force, so as to be applicable to an article of commerce purchased before its promulgation.

I must make it clear that the 1,381 bundles shipped to Manila on the ship mentioned are a part of the 2,500 bought in this port of Legaspi for the gentlemen whose names appear in the accompanying statement or note, which is a literal copy of the one presented by me voluntarily on October 17th last to the delegado then in office, Señor Fulgencio Contreras.

Having then paid into the treasury of the government the sum of $1,381, to which the 5 per cent export duty amounted, in consequence of the demand of the present delegado, Señor Cruz, I beg of the general to please declare exempt from said payment of duty the 2,500 bundles acquired before the establishing of this new impost, or otherwise to make a proper decision to settle said question, which is not clear to me.   It is justice that I beg.

Legaspi, December 26, 1898.

J. H. OSMOND.

No. 7.

OFFICE OF THE SECRETARY OF THE TREASURY,
Malolos, February 2, 1899.

DECREE.

Referring to the petition presented by Mr. J. H. Osmond, a British subject and representative of Messrs. Smith, Bell & Company, a business firm of Manila, appealing from the judgment rendered by the delegado de marina of the port of Legaspi, wherein he requests the repayment of $1,085, paid into said office of the delegado de marina, which impost is equivalent to 5 per cent of the value of 1,085 bundles of hemp, as an export duty, in conformity with the decree of November 17th last, alleging that these goods had been acquired before the promulgation of said decree.

Whereas in view of the fact that the payment in question must be demanded upon the article on which imposed in the act of loading same on the ship, which occurred on December 9, while the decree mentioned was already in force, as is shown by the receipt No. 15; and inasmuch as in deciding the matter the time of acquisition should not be taken into consideration, for the reason that the decree in question has no bearing whatever upon the time of acquisition of the article of commerce through legal means recognized by the civil and commercial codes now in force provisionally; while on the other hand, the decree creates a customs tax recognized and approved by all civilized nations.   Upon the recommendation of the secretary of the treasury, I hereby declare that there are no grounds for repaying the sum of

$1,085, requested by the representative of Messrs. Smith, Bell & Company, Mr. J. H. Osmond, who will be notified of this decree.

MARIANO TRIAS, *Secretary.*

—— ——,
President of the Republic.

NOTE.—On this same date the instructions contained in the above decree were complied with by sending a complete notification to the interested party through the jefe de marina of the port of Legaspi. In witness whereof I sign this.

SIMEON SORIANO.

No. 8.

(This is exactly the same as the preceding, except that it refers to $1,381, impost on 1,381 bundles of hemp, shipped on December 26th, as shown by receipt No. 24.—Translator.)

Ma.

NOTE ON RELATIONS WITH THE INSURGENTS OF CERTAIN FIRMS ENGAGED IN TRADE IN SAMAR.

In describing the methods of the government instituted by Emilio Aguinaldo and his followers in the Philippines from sources which have survived the vicissitudes of war, there are, as is to be expected, periods of time and portions of territory which are not covered by documents. This does not mean that no documents existed, but merely that they have been destroyed or have not reached this office. There are, however, places where for certain periods the documentary evidence relating to certain subjects is complete. For example, a number of depositions taken by the judge-advocate of the Department of the Visayas and other officers in Sámar during 1901 are on file in the Bureau of Insular Affairs of the War Department (under file No. 5431), which show how Lucban, commanding the insurgents in Samar, was able to obtain supplies of rice and money to keep up his guerilla warfare by the taxes he collected upon the sale of hemp (abacá) to foreign merchants trading in that island. The evidence led the United States military authorities to expel from Sámar on October 7, 1901, Mr. Gibson, agent for Warner, Barnes & Co., and Mr. Easton, agent for Smith, Bell & Co., and permission to trade in Samar was refused to the firms they represented until trade was reopened with Samar on May 15, 1902. There was, however, no general trade permitted with that island before the latter date.

This expulsion was on account of what appeared conclusive evidence of these firms engaging in contraband trade with and paying taxes to the insurgents in that island. It may be well to state that Mr. Easton made an affidavit before the acting British consul in Manila that he had in no way aided the insurgents and that a full account of the firm's transactions had been forwarded to Manila. A further affidavit by him was made before the judge-advocate at Catbalogan that no clandestine sales had been made and no rice sent or money paid out of

86

Catbalogan without the permission of the United States military authorities.

The reports of examinations of persons in Sámar from which these extracts were made are of considerable scope and cover subjects which do not bear upon the case in issue. These extracts are of interest as showing the relations of agents of foreign trading companies in Manila with the insurgents in Sámar during the period of hostilities before October, 1901.

TRANSLATION OF LETTERS CAPTURED AT DAGUPAN.

[P. I. R. Originals filed 49–3.]

There is a letter head which says: "Smith, Bell & Co., Manila, Cebú, Iloilo. Telegraphic address: Bell, Manila."

MANILA, *December 9, 1898.*

To the honorable Señor EMILIO AGUINALDO,
    President of the revolutionary government of the Philippines.

HONORABLE SIR: We desire to establish an agency of our house at Calbayog, and must send to represent us Mr. W. Easton, a person who has our confidence, and for whom we will stand as sponsors.

For the personal safety of that gentleman, as well as for the security of our interests, we request you to be so kind as to recommend him to the jefes locales of Calbayog; not only that they may pay attention to him, but also that they may permit him to engage in the business that takes him there, to the advantage of all.

You will receive the thanks, if you have the kindness to grant this favor, of those who declare themselves with the greatest consideration, most sincerely your servants, who kiss your hand,
    (Signed)   SMITH BELL CO.

The undersigned, English merchants established in this town, hereby declare that there goes to the province of Samar, for business purely mercantile, their assistant, Mr. W. Easton, a person who enjoys their most complete confidence, and for whom they stand as sponsors. They request the local government to allow him to travel freely.

Manila, December 9, 1898.
    (Signed)   SMITH, BELL & Co., *Manila.*

There is a stamp which says: "Smith, Bell & Co., Manila."

[Translation.]

[P. I. R. Original filed 259–1.]

(Jefatura Superior Militar de Leyte y Sámar. War Department Number 218. E/R. G. No. 284—1.)

Enclosed I send you statement, accompanied by vouchers, of the source of the funds of this province of Samar, not being able to do it with that of Leyte on account of its having been retained there, and to-day I ask for it, and as soon as possible I will have the honor of forwarding it to your office, with the list of names of the war-tax payers of each town, which I likewise order prepared to-day by the respective local authorities.

God keep you many years.

[SEAL.]   VICENTE LUCBAN.

CATBALOGAN, 17 March, '99·

(Jefaᵗᵃ Supʳ Milᵗʳ Camˢ Catandˢ Sámar y Leyte.)
Secretary of finance of the government of the Philippine republic.

[Endorsement.]

TARLAC, 26 June, 1899.

To the proper bureau for the necessary action to turn amounts involved into the treasury.

———

POLITICAL-MILITARY GOVERNMENT, SÁMAR.

To the SECRETARY OF THE TREASURY
OF THE PHILIPPINE REPUBLIC.

SIR: Since the beginning of April last I have had the honor of sending to your office by Mr. Francisco Enaje the sum of $78,000 and odd belonging to funds of the province of Leyte, and $100,000 from this province of Sámar, making a total of $178,000 and odd. I do not know whether you have received them as yet or not. I have on hand now the sum of $47,597.18, as you will see by the accounts herewith, and I should like to be informed by that office as to the manner of remitting same, as I don't like to send drafts on Warner-Barnes.

God guard you many years.

Calbayog, July 8, 1899.

VICENTE LUCBAN,
Political-Military Governor.

———

On November 1, 1901, a board of officers met at Catbalogan, Sámar, P. I., pursuant to field orders, No. 84, headquarters Department of the Visayas, Cebú, P. I., October 31, 1901, to determine the legitimate owners of certain hemp at Catbalogan, and to recommend the disposition to be made of it. The firm of Smith, Bell & Co. was represented at Catbalogan by Mr. Walter Easton, and the firm of Warner, Barnes & Co. by Mr. John H. Gibson, who was succeeded about September 1, 1901, by Mr. G. W. Brown.

The said hemp had apparently been purchased by these agents. In all the board listed some 1,481 piculs of hemp belonging to Warner, Barnes & Co., and 1,920 piculs of hemp belonging to Smith, Bell & Co.

The board having taken testimony in the case, was of the following opinion and made the following recommendation:

" * * * The board further found that the purchasing agents of both of the above-mentioned firms were directed to purchase and did actually purchase all of the hemp possible from all persons who possessed it, whether insurgents or not; and, second, that it was understood and agreed between the parties selling and purchasing, and the purchasing agents as well, that a tax of a certain (10) per cent was to be paid to the insurgents on all hemp purchased or shipped out of the island of

Sámar, and that such tax was actually paid, or agreed to be paid, on all hemp so purchased as aforesaid.

"The board therefore recommends that all the hemp purchased by the above-mentioned firms, and now stored as stated, be confiscated and sold and the proceeds thereof be placed to the credit of the United States.

"The board further recommends the sale to be made at the best price that can be obtained."

Interview with Vicente Jasminez, August 31, 1901.

By Maj. E. F. Glenn, Fifth Infantry.

Q. What office were you holding with the Filipino government until the time you were arrested?—A. I was delegad(o) of police before; appointed by Lucban.

Q. What date were you appointed?—A. In the month of October last.

* * * * * * *

Q. How much does Walter (Warner), Barnes & Co. contribute?—A. They give ten of rice for each clerk, and they have houses in Catbalogan, Calbayog, Paranas, and Miabong.

Q. I want to know how much they contribute in rice and money in Catbalogan.—A. As I said, they pay ten picos for each clerk.

Q. Is that right?—A. Yes, sir.

Q. Who collects this from them?—A. Loreccio Bris and Norberto Igua.

Q. How many clerks has he that he pays for in Catbalogan?—A. Three in the town and also for all they have in the branch houses; and they pay $10 a month also for each.

* * * * * *

TARANGNAN, SÁMAR, P. I., *October 7, 1901.*

Ciriago Alcazar to Capt. F. H. Schoeffel, Ninth Infantry.

Q. Who has been furnishing rice to the insurrection from Catbalogan?—A. The Filipino government bought it from the English.

Q. What English?—A. Mr. Scott and Mr. Donsey.

Q. Who did Donsey represent?—A. Warner, Barnes.

Q. Who was Mr. Scott agent for?—A. Warner, Barnes.

Who was the representative of Smith, Bell & Co.?—A. Mr. Easton.

Q. How much did they buy of Easton?—A. Very much.

Q. Where did Warner, Barnes & Co. buy the rice they brought into Catbalogan?—A. Tacloban and Manila.

Q. How much did Warner, Barnes & Co. have to pay insurrecto government, and how did they pay it?—A. I do not know. It was a secret between them.

Q. How much did they have to pay the insurrectos for every arroba of hemp they secured?—A. Two cents first, and now 10 cents.

* * * * * * * *

Q. How much money did Lucban send you to build traps around Dapdap?—A. Lucban sent over $200 to the teniente of barrio Dapdap.

Q. How much did you get to work?—A. Nothing. I gave the teniente of the barrio $30 (pesos).

Q. What is the name of the teniente?—A. Urbano.

Q. Where did the teniente use that money to build traps?—A. In all of the roads.

Q. In what town or barrio?—A. Roads of the barrio Dapdap and in the lands (farms).

Q. When did you give him the money?—A. In August. About this time a man of Captain Schoeffel's company was killed by one of these traps at Dapdap.

* * * * * * *

Q. What authority did you have for paying money into the insurrectos?—A. I had a commission.

Q. Of whom?—A. Lucban.

Q. When did you make this arrangement with Lucban?—A. In March.

Extracts of the deposition of Silvestre García, Spaniard, taken by Maj. E. F. Glenn, Fifth Infantry, judge-advocate, Department of the Visayas, Catbalogan, Sámar, P. I., October 24, 1901.

* * * * * * *

Q. I want to know about this hemp bought of Smith, Bell & Co., the rice you bought, etc.—A. During this year I only bought 175 picos, which was contracted with Apolonio Daza. I did not take any rice at all from the house.

Q. Where did you get this hemp? Where did he get it from?—A. I have information that a great deal of abacá came from Tarangnan, Silanganan, and some other points of this coast.

Q. How much did you have to pay for the hemp?—A. I bought the hemp from Apolonio at $14 per pico, and I contracted with Smith, Bell & Co. for $14.25 per pico.

Q. Who paid the tax of the insurgent government of 10 per cent, you, yourself, or who?—A. I know that there was an order from Lucban to pay 10 per cent per pico for abacá coming out of Sámar. I did not pay any tax for that abacá, because I contracted for it at the certain price of $14. I received the abacá in accordance with the account.

Q. Then the man who contracted with you had already paid this tax of 10 per cent, had he?—A. I supposed that he paid the tax, because that was the order of all of the towns.

Q. I want to know who pays this tax or impost of 10 per cent. Does the man who brings the abacá to sell or the agent who buys it— who does pay it?—A. In all of the towns it is customary for the purchaser to pay the tax to the tribunals.

Q. If I understand you correctly, then, the practice was when a purchaser bought some hemp he reserved from the purchase price 10 per cent?—A. Yes, sir; and delivered it to the jefe local——

Q. What becomes of this tax that is collected by the tribunals?— A. The order of Lucban was to send to him all of the money collected——

Q. Is it a fact or not, a generally known fact, among purchasers that buy hemp in this island that they are subject to a tax of 10 per cent?—A. Yes, sir; because in October last year I was taken a prisoner in Matinginao when it was published. They were speaking about this order that all of the people of the town must pay 10 per cent on the abacá.

Q. Do you know it to be a fact that the firm of Warner, Barnes & Co., and the firm of Smith, Bell & Co., Tabacalera Company, and other firms buying hemp have to pay the tax of 10 per cent?—A. I heard formerly, and also since I have been a prisoner, that the houses used to pay contributions for the mountains—for the revolution.

Q. What I want to know is if these firms must have known of this order because of its having been so general?—A. I have not been in business with the houses and I do not know, but have heard in Tarangnan from two persons that they used to pay and the houses paid also. I do not know about here in Catbalogan, because I have not been here for six months.

Q. What was it you heard these men had to pay?—A. I do not know how much they paid on the rice, but on abacá I know that it was the custom to pay 10 per cent, because the order of Lucban said that all the abacá coming from Sámar must pay.

Q. Who has been furnishing the rice that has gone out to the insurrectos?—A. Each town has a particular local chief to take charge of collections and everything.

Q. Who furnished the rice that came in?—A. I have heard from people who bought the rice that it was from the Chinos, because the Chinos sold cheaper.

The witness being duly sworn, declares the foregoing facts are the truth.

CATBALOGAN, SÁMAR, P. I.,
October 25, 1901. (Night.)

J. R. C. Mariano Froilan. (Calbiga.)

Q. Where do you live?—A. In Calbiga; I have lived there twenty years. I have a store and buy abacá and sell rice and other things. Up to May I bought 100 picos of abacá for Warner, Barnes & Co. I had orders from Gibson to not pay more than 2 pesos on each pico to the insurrecto collectors. Gibson gave me a letter saying to buy from anybody I could, whether they were insurrectos or not. I have now in my house 100 picos in Calbiga. I reported to Mr. Gibson that I had deposited 100 picos. I told Gibson that I had paid this 2 pesos on each pico; he said: "All right." The books of Gibson show that I had an account.

Gibson gave me 1,000 pesos and 200 cavanes of rice and some goods, which were converted into money and invested in abacá.

(NOTE.—It is evidence that Generoso Almazán sent abacá to this same Froilan on his casco from Bató, receiving back in exchange pico for pico. *Vide* statement Feliciano Figueroa.)

I had no salary. My profits came from buying rice from the house at a lower price than I sold it; also in selling them abacá for more than it cost me. Prior to May I had a small store. José Monfort, an

-agent of Warner, Barnes & Co., came to my store. He found that I was buying rice and abacá in small quantities. Monfort told Gibson that I was buying abacá and then Gibson sent for me. I never had any conversation with Monfort; he came to my store to sell goods. He was an agent of Warner, Barnes & Co.

(NOTE.—Among other transactions, it would appear from the foregoing that José Monfort was engaged by Gibson to go about establishing branch agencies, selecting "that kind of persons," as Monfort calls insurrecto sympathizers, who, he says, were the only sort employed. He may have established others in the same way.)

Froilan said that he had in his house books showing list of all insurrectos he bought hemp from.

CATBALOGAN, SÁMAR, P. I., *October 26, 1901.*

Pablo Benjamin Cinco, President Federal Party, Calbiga, to Color Sergeant Stevens, First U. S. Infantry.

Q. Did you have a conversation with Gabino Hilbano, of Villareal, about the imposts which the agents of Smith, Bell & Co. had to pay on the abacá?—A. Yes.

Q. When?—About June 30.

Q. Where?—A. In Villareal.

Q. What did you say to him at that time about the imposts on abacá paid by the agents of Smith, Bell & Co.?—A. I told him: "The merchants of the Englishmen do not have to pay to the collectors nor the presidentes, because, as Generoso Almazán has told me, all of the duties of the house do not have to be paid to the presidentes, because Lucban told him (Generoso) that the collectors and the presidentes are not authorized to collect the percentage, because the general (Lucban) would look out for the collection from the agent of Smith, Bell & Co., Mr. Easton." I told him also that Mr. Easton had sent messengers through four men to the mountains to General Lucban. I told him that these letters were with regard to the payment of the impost by Easton.

CATBALOGAN, SÁMAR, P. I., *October 26, 1901.*

Estevan Figueroa, presidente of Calbiga, to Maj. E. F. Glenn, Fifth Infantry, A. J. A., judge-advocate, Department of Visayas.

Q. What office have you been holding this year?—A. I am presidente of Calbiga.

Q. Have you been in charge of the collection of the 10 per cent impost for the insurrectos on the abacá that goes out?—A. Formerly; but not this year.

Q. Why not this year? There has been over four thousand picos sent out on which you have not collected; why not?—A. I was afraid of the Americans.

Q. Did you collect the abacá tax on the abacá of the English firms?—A. No, sir.

Q. Why not?—A. The Englishmen (Gibson and Easton) told me that they would keep the agreement with Lucban when they could see him.

Q. Where were you when they told you this?—A. In Calbiga.

Q. What date was this?—A. The 6th of May.

Q. This year?—A. Yes, sir.

Q. Did you ever have any other conversation with these people?—A. No more.

Q. Where did you have this conversation, and who was present?—A. In my house; and they two were there only.

Q. Give the names of the persons who were actually present.—A. Myself, Mr. Easton, and Mr. Gibson.

* * * * * * *

Q. Do you know Generoso Almazán?—A. Yes, sir.

Q. Did you ever have any conversation with him about this impost of the agents of the Englishmen?—A. Yes, sir.

* * * * * * *

Q. What was the conversation you had?—A. He said to me, "I am authorized to collect all of the contributions of the agents now, the presidentes of the towns have nothing to do with it, now that there are American forces. I wish to meet the Englishmen to arrange the accounts about the abacá at Catbalogan." I do not know about the end of the matter, because Almazán came here with the presidente of the Federal party.

* * * * * * *

Q. Did he (Generoso Almazán) say that the English agents were to pay this tax to him as the commissioner of General Lucban?—A. He did not say that; he only said that he wanted to meet the Englishmen to settle the accounts for the abacá.

Q. Did you not say last night that you had a conversation in May with Generoso in which he said that he wanted to meet the Englishmen to arrange the agreement with them, and another conversation in June in which he said that he wanted to see the Englishmen to collect from them?—A. That is correct.

* * * * * * *

(At this juncture Generoso Almazán, former commissary officer (factor) of Lucban, was brought before the witness.)

Q. Is this the man?—A. Yes, sir.

CATBALOGAN, SÁMAR, P. I., *October 26, 1901.*

Gabino Hilbano, President Federal Party, Villareal.

The above-named Gabino Hilbano asked permission of the sergeant of the guard to see the judge-advocate, stating that he wished to make a certain declaration.

* * * * * * *

I will also say that Mr. Easton told me to buy all of the abacá that

I could find. He told me not to pay the contribution to the local chief as had been done before. He said that he would pay that and that he would take out the price of the contribution from the abacá.

He said, "Do not pay the contribution as we did before the detachment, the American detachment, went there, to the presidente, Buenaventura Lola." This Buenaventura Lola was the man who used to send the contributions to Generoso Almazán and Sabino Conge. During the time that the American detachment has been in Villareal I never left, and as the presidente of the Federal party I caused 280 men to present themselves. Lieutenant Snow can tell you whether this is true or not, because my house is in front of his.

* * * * * * *

Q. To whom did he (Mr. Easton) have to pay these contributions?— A. Before there was an American detachment in Villareal in June he had to pay to the presidente 1 peso on each pico of abacá and 1 real on each pico of rice.

Q. That tax of 1 peso does not account for the difference between the purchase and selling price?—A. It was their custom to pay here $14.50. and there at Tacloban to sell at $24 or $25 pesos, and we asked them many times why that was; and they answered, "That is the custom, because we have to pay contributions," and we never knew exactly what they did have to pay.

Q. In this first conversation you had with Mr. Easton, when he told you that he would look out for the impost on the abacá, whom did he say that he had an agreement to pay that to?—A. He told me to Lucban, and in truth I knew by rumors that he sent two men with letters to Lucban and those two men never came back.

* * * * * * *

CATBALOGAN, SÁMAR, P. I., *October 27, 1901.*

Generoso Almazan, factor and first lieutenant of military administration, to Maj. E. F. Glenn, Fifth Infantry, A. J. A., judge-advocate, Department Visayas.

Q. Where do you live?—A. In Salog, on the other side of the town.

Q. What office did you hold last year and up to June this year, with the insurrectos?—A. First lieutenant of the military administration (commissary department).

Q. What else?—A. That was all.

Q. Were you a commissioner of any kind for the collection of an impost or tax or anything of that sort for Lucban?—A. Yes, sir; I was appointed to collect from the local chiefs.

Q. Did you at any time have anything to do about making arrangements for the supply of rice that came in?—A. Yes, sir; I was a commissioner to send the rice.

Q. How was that arranged—how was it done?—A. I used to send the rice every week.

Q. Where did you get it?—A. I got it from Mr. Gibson when he sent it to me.

Q. Did you have any arrangement with Mr. Gibson about sending it?—A. By order of Lucban I went to Talolura to meet him.

Q. When did you go to Talulora to meet Gibson?—A. In November.
Q. Of last year?—A. Yes, sir.

*   *   *   *   *   *   *

Q. Where were you when you got this letter from Lucban directing you to go there and meet Messrs. Gibson and Easton.—A. In Bató.
Q. How did Lucban know Gibson and Easton would be at Talulora to meet you?—A. Surely (seguro), through letters between Lucban and Mr. Easton to go there and meet me.

*   *   *   *   *   *   *

Q. I want to know what else, if anything, you carried from General Lucban and presented to Messrs. Gibson and Easton. You mentioned orders just now; what were they?—A. Yes, sir; one letter that was as follows: "The bearer of this is in charge of receiving the rice, and he will designate for you the place where the rice must be sent." When I showed them the letter they asked me where they should send the rice, and I answered them: "To Bató."
Q. Did they, pursuant to this agreement, deliver any rice or not?—A. They told me they would send it.
Q. Did they send it?—A. Yes, sir.
Q. Tell me where Mr. Gibson sent it, and how much, and when.—A. Gibson sent first on the 15th of November, 25 sacks; on the 19th, 20 sacks; afterwards, on the 4th of December, 10 sacks; on the 16th of December, 30 sacks; and afterwards, 5 sacks on the 28th of December. That is all from Gibson.
Q. Did Mr. Easton send any under that agreement; and if so, where did he send it from, how much, and when?—A. He sent from Mualbual on the 3d of January, this year, 20 sacks; on the 14th of January, 15 sacks; on the 18th of January, 25 sacks; and February 6, 10 sacks.
Q. Did you have any definite arrangement as to any definite amount these people were to send?—A. Yes, sir; for each year each one was to furnish 500 sacks.
Q. They were each one to furnish 500 sacks a year for your center?—A. Yes, sir.

*   *   *   *   *   *   *

Q. Who used this rice when it got to Masac-pasac?—A. The insurrectos. They had a camp there.

CATBALOGAN, SÁMAR, P. I., *October 28, 1901.*

Feliciano Figueroa, formerly delegate of police, and at time of arrest presidente of Calbiga. Hemp sold to W. B. & Co.

Prior to March this year was engaged in a partnership with Rafáel Latorre. Figueroa had $120 and two carabao, which he sold for 80 pesos, making a capital of $200; Rafael had an equal amount, and with this $400 they bought some 50 picos of hemp from Biti and Unoy, insurrectos, who brought it from the vicinity of Bató.

Figueroa and Latorre paid the 10 per cent impost on this hemp to Presidente Esteban Figueroa.

They sold it to Mariano Froilán, agent at Calbiga, of Warner, Barnes & Co. (Gibson), who knew whence it came and that the tax had been paid on it.

In March this partnership between Figueroa and Latorre was ended. Figueroa then came to Catbalogan with Mariano Froilán. They called upon Gibson, who loaned 600 pesos to Froilán with the knowledge that Froilán was borrowing it to relend to Feliciano Figueroa, who was present at the transaction. On this occasion Gibson told Figueroa personally to "buy hemp wherever you can and from anybody you can, whether they are insurrectos or not," or words to that effect.

With this 600 pesos borrowed from Gibson, Feliciano Figueroa bought about 50 picos of hemp, which was delivered to and is now deposited in the house of Mariano Froilán, agent of Gibson at Calbiga. It is, by Figueroa's admission, the property of Gibson, as it was purchased with his money.

Figueroa says that he did not pay the tax on this last amount, purchased with the Gibson money, because in June, he says, June 6, Generoso Almazán was in Calbiga and told him in the house of Pablo Benjamin Cinco that Gibson and Easton had written to Lucban agreeing to pay the taxes imposed upon their agents personally. This was after the meeting mentioned by Alejandro Sevarre, Pablo B. Cinco, Esteban Figueroa, and Generoso himself. They were all still in Cinco's house.

CATBALOGAN, SÁMAR, P. I., *October 24, 1901.*—(Night.)

Alejandro Sevarre to Lieutenant Hoover

I live in Calbiga, where I have a little store, and used to buy abacá in small quantities. In February Mr. Easton sent for me and promised me a salary of $60 a month to buy abacá in Calbiga. I bought about 200 picos from the people of the town.

Angel Figueroa sold me 40 picos at $13.50. I paid the tax of 10 per cent on this to the presidente, Esteban Figueroa, brother of the man I bought the 40 picos from.

Biti and Unoy or Onoy, two brothers, insurrectos, who live in Manjangcao, sold this to Angel Figueroa. I know that Biti and Unoy were insurrectos, because Capitan Esteban Figueroa used them as carriers of the rice and money he sent to Bató to Generoso Almazán.

This 40 picos of hemp was bought from Angel in April, and belongs to Mr. Easton, although it was not delivered to him. It is in his books. Mr. Easton knows the tax was paid. He knew that all hemp coming from the mountains was insurrecto hemp. It was customary to pay all the time until the Americans arrived.

Mr. Easton told me to go up there and buy all the abacá I could, in any way I could. I understand the words, "Buy all the abacá you can, in any way you can," to mean I was to buy from the town or mountains and pay the tax.

Now on deposit.—I have over 200 picos belonging to Mr. Easton on deposit, and I have advanced money for about 100 more to people who have it in small quantities. Mr. Easton sent me about 300 picos of rice, and I sold the rice and bought abacá with the proceeds.

(NOTE.—This was probably the rice that was exchanged at Calbiga for hemp that came from Bató in the boat of Generoso Almazán, the insurrecto commissary officer, to whom rice was sent in exchange, pico for pico. *Vide* statement of Feliciano Figueroa.)

Before ports closed, from February to May, bought 600 or 700 picos. All this with Easton's money. Taxes on all this were paid to Figueroa, save some that Esteban Figueroa agreed to wait for. This was bought from Angel Figueroa and "Ponso." All Angel and Ponso sold him came from mountains. It was impossible to buy hemp in town, and in the mountains everybody was insurrectos. Mr. Easton knew tax was paid, because he knew no one could get abacá out without paying the impost.

To Alejandro Sevarre.

Q. Repeat to the witness (Pablo B. Cinco) what you said that you, Generoso, say in his house.—A. He said that "You don't have to collect the contributions on the abacá, because the Englishmen have written letters to Lucban."

To Pablo B. Cinco.

Q. The presidente (Esteban Figueroa) recollects the substance of what was said just as this man has stated. Do you remember anything of it?—A. I remember now that he said the Englishmen wrote some letters to the mountains.

To Generoso Almazin.

Q. Do you remember that conversation now that three men have recalled it to you?—A. Yes, sir; I remember now. Lucban told me that I did not need to collect any contributions on abacá because he had letters from the Englishmen.

Q. That you did not have to collect contributions from whom?—A. That I did not have to collect the 10 per cent on abacá.

Q. From whom?—A. He said that I did not need to collect because he had letters from the Englishmen.

Q. Did he say what was in the letters?—A. No; Lucban only told me that he had some letters.

CATBALOGAN, SÁMAR, P. I., *October 30, 1901.*

José Monfort (Spaniard) to Edwin F. Glenn, major Fifth Infantry A. J. A., judge-advocate, department Visayas.

Q. I have information that in the month of June Mr. Easton, the agent of Smith, Bell & Co., wrote to Lucban?—A. It is true.

Q. I have heard that in this letter he said that he would pay the impost on abacá?—A. When I was in Matuginao, Lucban said that Easton had written him a letter in which he said that he wanted all the abacá outside the American lines, and that he would pay a sufficiently large contribution if Lucban did not molest or interfere with the purchasers (personas) that Mr. Easton sent out after it.

Q. Was this the same letter that arranged for Gibson also?—A. No; because I think that he and Gibson had an understanding some

time before that. When the Americans arrived here I think that Mr.
Easton had a slight misunderstanding with Lucban, and as a result of
this disagreement Mr. Easton had considerable trouble in securing
abacá. He determined to write him this letter. He sent the first
letter by two messengers, but on account of this misunderstanding
Lucban took them prisoners, and they were kept in this condition
until they could escape, and it was for this reason that he wrote the
second letter. The first letter he sent by Pepe Muño, and the second
by laborers that he has here. I do not recall their names.

Q. Could you remember them if you heard them?—A. I think so.

Q. Were they Mariano Palaspas and one Fermin?—A. Yes; those
are the men; I was talking to them in Matuginao. They carried the
second letter.

Q. What date did he send this—the last one?—A. Two or three
months before the Twenty-ninth Infantry went away.

Q. This letter was about the impost?—A. Yes, sir.

Q. What date was that?—A. Before the going away of the Twenty-
ninth; I think it was in May.

Q. Who wrote this letter—himself or his clerks?—A. He himself.
I saw the letter in the hands of General Lucban. I did not read it,
but recognized the handwriting. I saw the signature of Easton; it
was his.

Q. When did you see it?—A. I was there in the month of May; I
left the 23d of May.

Q. I want to know exactly how these Englishmen paid this tax; did
they pay it themselves, or how?—A. I know that they—that these
people must have arranged this before the arrival of the Americans,
because when I was in the camp of Lucban I knew that he had received
letters from them. You can prove that, because all of the agents
employed were aiding the insurrectos, and they looked for and
employed that kind of persons, and that is the reason why their business is not interfered with by the people of the mountains. (José
Monfort was one of "that kind of persons." He was an agent.)

Q. But all of these people have to pay 10 per cent?—A. Yes, sir;
that is true.

Q. I have information that until April those agents in Calbiga and
other places paid this tax.—A. Up to the last moment they paid.
Some days before I was arrested I was talking with Mariano Froilan
in the house of Gibson, and he told me that he had paid large contributions in this way to the agent of Francisco Rafael.

(Francisco Rafael was the jefe of the Masac-pasac—Catbalogan—
Center.)

CATBALOGAN, SÁMAR, P. I., *October 31, 1901.*

Domingo Cui, president of Tarangnan, to Maj. E. F. Glenn, Fifth
Infantry, A. J. A., judge-advocate Department Visayas.

Q. What is your name?—A. Domingo Cuí.

Q. Where do you live?—A. In Tarangnan.

Q. What is your business?—A. Merchant.

Q. Were you an agent for anyone this year?—A. August and September I was the agent (comerciante) of Smith, Bell & Co.

Q. Were you an agent of either of the English houses before that this year?—A. No, sir.

Q. What were you doing before that?—A. I had a little store.

*　　*　　*　　*　　*　　*　　*

Q. What were your instructions from Smith, Bell & Co. as to where you should purchase and from whom?—A. They only ordered me to exchange goods for goods.

Q. Did he tell you to buy from any particular person?—A. Only to buy from everybody.

Q. I have been informed that for two or three years past Lucban has had an order requiring a certain percentage to be collected on abacá and other goods going out of this island; is that trué or not?—A. Yes, sir; 10 per cent.

Q. And this has been collected regularly by the local presidentes or parties designated by Lucban; is that true?—A. Yes, sir.

Q. And the rule was that the presidentes were responsible ordinarily; is that true?—A. Yes, sir; the local chiefs.

Q. Was this information general, so that all purchasers of abacá knew of it?—A. Yes, sir.

Q. Was it so general that the agents of Smith, Bell, and Warner, Barnes—that is, Easton and Gibson—must have known of this?—A. Yes, sir; they knew it.

Q. Do you know personally that they knew it, aside from the general knowledge; for instance, do you know that Mr. Easton knew it?—A. Yes, sir; because all of the world knew it.

Q. As a matter of fact, who paid this in your dealings with Easton? Did you pay this or Mr. Easton?—A. I have not paid yet, but Mr. Easton was responsible for that tax in the mountains.

Q. You know that Mr. Easton was responsible?—A. Yes, sir; the heads of the house were to send contributions to Lucban, so that Lucban did not molest any of their agents in the towns.

· Q. Do you know personally how this arrangement between the heads of the house and Lucban were made?—A. They themselves wrote to Lucban.

Q. The English heads wrote letters to Lucban?—A. Yes, sir; I knew that when I was a prisoner for eight months, because I did not give any contributions.

Q. Did you see these letters from either of these men?—A. In the conversation around his dinner table this Lucban himself told that the English houses paid this contribution.

*　　*　　*　　*

CATBALOGAN, SÁMAR, P. L, *November 1, 1901.*

Luis Moro (Spaniard), agent S. B. & Co., to Maj. E. F. Glenn, Fifth Infantry, A. J. A., judge-advocate Department Visayas.

Q. I have heard from a good many sources that General Lucban, in the time of the Spanish, imposed a tax of a certain per cent upon all the abacá that went out of Sámar, and that they continued to pay this up to very recently. I would like to know if that is true and all about it?—A. It is true.

Q. Was this of such general information that everybody was bound to know it?—A. Yes, sir.

Q. All the purchasers of abacá knew it?—A. Yes, sir; everybody, and the small merchants also.

Q. Then the agents of Warner, Barnes & Smith Bell here must have known of it?—A. The houses here paid that impost for all of the abacá and rice coming from Manila or going there, and on large quantities the impost was 5 per cent.

Q. How do you know of their paying 5 per cent, when the rule was 10 per cent?—A. This 5 per cent was for large quantities of rice that came in. I am not sure, but I believe it was for that reason. And the agents did not pay any tax on that because the heads of the houses paid all of it. When large boats came here they paid the taxes.

Q. How did they pay this tax?—A. The collectors were the presidentes of the towns.

Q. Can you tell me when the agents or persons, the purchasers of the English houses paid this impost—men like yourself, Monfort, and García? I have heard that some time this year—April or May—they quit paying and another method was arranged.—A. In the towns occupied by the Americans they quit paying openly when the Americans arrived, but paid it secretly; but in towns that were not occupied they continued to pay.

Q. I have been told that about April of this year, Mr. Easton made some special arrangement which relieved his purchasers, like yourself and others, in the different districts from paying. Can you tell anything about this?—A. I do not know about that, because I did not commence until July, when I went to Mutiong. When I went to Mutiong he (Easton) said to me: "With respect to the contributions or impost you do not need to pay, and if they demand that of you, you say to them that I have an agreement about this with General Lucban, and when the abacá comes to me it is when I pay the taxes."

Q. Have you heard anything about a letter having been sent about the time I mention—May or April—some time about then, by Mr. Easton to Lucban, about paying this tax?—A. I know that he sent a messenger (despacho), but the contents I can not tell you, because I was a simple dependiente expedicionario; but when I was in Mutiong one of the despachos presented himself, and that man was the one who told me of this letter.

*　　　*　　　*

Manuel A. de Ojeda (written statement).

I am convinced that the rice sent by the house of Warner, Barnes of Calbayog to the Visitas of Santo Niño, Almagro or Talag and San Antonio, for the dependientes or merchants that were there, Pablo Borromeo, Leoncio Lamajan, and Pedro Francisco, was, for the greater part, left in the country of the insurrection, and that the abacá bought came from the same place, and that these merchants had to be officers, or to pay a contribution to insurgents, because, if not that, they would not be able to negotiate in said places, nor in others where there was no armed detachment.

I also believe that this business has contributed to the sustenance of the insurrection, because if they had not had rice, money, and clothes they would not have been able to live in the country.

I know that a contribution was paid on rice and abacá, because I was told so by Mr. Gibson one day when we were talking about business. He was sorry afterwards for having told me, not having any confidence in me.

I know that the lorcha, *Maud*, of the house of Warner, Barnes & Co., made two voyages to the islands of Liban, Cauayan, Maripipi, and Talagib at the end of July or the beginning of August, 1900, carrying rice, anisado, and other effects. All of the rice and part of the other effects were sold, and she returned with almost a complete cargo of abacá, which was discharged in the warehouse of the firm.

On the second voyage she carried rice and other effects, and returned, having sold one part of it and bringing less abacá than on the former voyage.

At the end of October or the beginning of November of the same year, Gibson went to the visita of Sto. Niño, on board the *San Bernardino*, carrying rice, and money which I saw taken from the safe, and by the bulk it seemed to me to be about 4,000 pesos. He was there about six days, and returned with abacá.

At the end of the same month, November, or the beginning of December, the steamer *San Bernardino* went to San Antonio and took abacá, contracted with Pedro Francisco, and I believe he paid 3,000 pesos in advance.

Moreover, other small boats have gone to the same islands, as launches and the steamer *Lotus*, with rice in small quantities, and also I know that a launch went from the house of Smith, Bell that carried rice and returned with about 50 picos of abacá, but I do not remember the date.

One day, as I was near the desk where the bookkeeper worked, it struck me to look at the account headed with the title: "Gobierno revolucionario" (revolutionary government); I looked and saw that it had a balance of more than 5,000 pesos in favor of the said "Gobierno," and that it was a contribution not yet paid.

＊   ＊   ＊   ＊   ＊

Catbalogan, 12 of November, 1901.

      (Signed) MANUEL A. DE OJEDA.

NOTE.—Printed on page 42 of document Court of Claims, Nos. 22757 and 22758. (Original on file Bureau of Insular Affairs.)

[P. I. R. Filed No. 259–1.]

Sámar funds to forward to office.

Draft against A. D. Suntian	$1,500.00
Draft against W. Barnes	2,000.00
Do	2,500.00
Bills, Filipino Bank	120.00
Draft against Aldecoa & Co	12,302.50
In gold, $4 and $2	1,024.66
Draft against W. Barnes & Co	4,764.66
Sum total	24,211.16

Katbalogan, 15 March, 1899.

[SEAL.]

        VICENTE LUKBAN.

(Jefat* Sup* Mil*, Kam* Katand*, Samar and Leyte.)

Funds of Samar and Leyte for the office, delivered to Mr. Enaje.

Dates of drafts.			In favor of—	Against—	Num-ber of draft.	Amounts.	
Day.	Month.	Year.				Dollars.	Cents.
25	Oct ...	1898	Carlos Navarro..............	A. D. Suntian.........	31	1,500	....
20	Feb...	1899	W. Barnes, Kalbayog.......	W. Barnes	181	2,500	....
16	Feb...	1899	W. Barnes, Paranas..........	.....do	34	2,000	....
23	Feb...	1899	W. Barnes, Barugo...........	.....do	135	6,015	15
23	Feb...	1899	.....do	.....do	136	2,810	28
23	Feb...	1899	.....do	.....do	137	4,766	67
11	Feb...	1899	Sr. Escaño, Malitbog.......	Aldecoa & Co..........	137	49,899	08
11	Feb...	1899	Sr. Escaño, Malitbog.......	.....do	137	33,509	58
			Bills, Banco Filipino, for $10.00	....	137	130	58
			Gold coins, $4 and $2	....	....	1,024	58
			Sum total.............	....	....	104,154	76

Received.

FRANCISCO ENAJE.

Katbalogan, 15th of March, 1899.

Delivered.

[SEAL.]

LUKBAN.

(Jefat^a Sup^r Mil^r, Kam^a Katand^a, Samar y Leyte.)

(NOTE.—The Spanish authorities translated the Tagalo " K " by using " C." In consequence the same name of a place or person is sometimes spelled with a " K " and sometimes with a " C."—J. R. M. T.)

O

CPSIA information can be obtained
at www.ICGtesting.com
Printed in the USA
LVOW10s0542160817

545177LV00020B/1284/P